# EYES OF THE SPIRIT

## THE AUTHOR

Colum Hayward is a grandson of Grace Cooke,
through whom the White Eagle teaching was
given. Born in 1952, he was brought up at New
Lands, country centre of the White Eagle Lodge,
but spent eight years at Cambridge University,
gaining both a first degree and a Ph.D. in English
Literature. He teaches meditation and is the
administrator of the London Centre of the White
Eagle Lodge. His hobbies include climbing and
mountaineering.

# Eyes of the Spirit

## Working with a spiritual teacher

COLUM HAYWARD

THE WHITE EAGLE PUBLISHING TRUST

NEW LANDS · LISS · HAMPSHIRE · ENGLAND

First published December 1997
Updated and reprinted, August 1999
© The White Eagle Publishing Trust, 1997

British Library Cataloguing-in-Publication Data
A catalogue record for this book is available from the British Library

ISBN 0-85487-103-9

Set in Garamond by the publisher and printed and bound in Great Britain
at the University Press, Cambridge

## CONTENTS

# Introduction

Although this book is subtitled 'working with a spiritual teacher', a little more than a discourse on how to make best use of a teacher is intended. First, it is to a specific teacher that I shall refer throughout: White Eagle, the spirit guide of Grace Cooke. His 'Lodge', the home and centre of his teaching, has been in existence since 1936, and has provided space and inspiration for many people to unfold their gifts during that time. The shared purpose there causes it often to be called 'the White Eagle *work*'; it then has the sense of a teaching framework too.

Such an opening statement might imply that my intention is to set out the guidance of one particular teacher and ask you to accept it. Although I do not allude to other teachers beside White Eagle except cursorily, there is a little more detachment in this book than might meet the eye. A teacher from spirit offers us a vision uncorrupted by the hustle and bustle of everyday life. Actually living the teaching is a different matter from giving it! The subtle counterpoint between what a teaching says, and how it can be lived out, is the real subject of the book. In this an explanation of the White Eagle Lodge as an organization is vital, because the Lodge is, among other things, a human experiment in living White Eagle's teaching. The teaching is the vision, the hope, the guiding star for those who live it; but those who live it are all of them human, and bring along with their aspiration all sorts of layers of difficulty which only the gentle influence of the teaching can (and does) shift. As a rider to this I should like to say, however, that I don't believe everyone who enjoys White Eagle's teaching has to commit themselves to being a member of the White Eagle Lodge.

White Eagle himself caused the Lodge to be set up, but not only because its services would provide an opportunity for him to give teaching: rather, that because the central platform of his teaching is brotherhood, that concept could only ever be learnt in practice. You cannot teach brotherhood, you can only provide circumstances in which it can be lived, and be an example of it. Up to a point, therefore, the Lodge itself is part of White Eagle's teaching, though it is the part which inevitably is the most affected by human interpretation!

It will also be apparent that my own relation to the teaching is a subject of the book: I hope usefully, because that human engagement is the point of contact between you, the reader, and me. I am not particularly wanting to put myself forward, but in order to be true in describing the fine play between hearing the teaching and living it, I have to speak from personal experience. That experience is sometimes utterly personal, and sometimes heavily dependent on my having been immersed in the White Eagle work from birth (Grace Cooke was my maternal grandmother). I hope that despite this dependence, it will always be clear that the views expressed are personal ones, and not necessarily what would have been put forward by another of White Eagle's workers.

I have gone quite deeply into the teaching in this book because it seemed most helpful not just to offer an introduction, but a commentary for those already familiar with it as well. The application of the mental faculty to something deeply heart-based will carry its limitations! There is no substitute in reading this book for the extraordinary feeling of love that one may have—of loving intelligence and deep human wisdom—when listening to a true voice from spirit.

The title 'Eyes of the Spirit' describes precisely what I think a teacher like White Eagle can provide for us. He is a teacher *from* *spirit*, and his perspective is different because of that. You can't *argue* with him over his teaching like you could with a physical teacher, but by the same token nothing he puts forward is dogmatic. In effect, he says on any issue, 'Would it help if you looked at it in this way?'; or, at most, 'From our perspective it looks like this'. To help you see from a better perspective is all he can do, but it is an enormous thing to be able to offer.

White Eagle once said, 'You are spirit: this is all you need to know'. Spirit is to him the essential part of us, the part that is completely undying and even unchanging. 'Soul' is the collection of impressions and understanding that we carry with us, the part that develops over more than just an earthly lifetime. His teaching is designed to remind us of the consciousness of *spirit* as not only our eternal reality but an ever-present one. My belief is that we really can see things from the same point of view as one who lives 'in the light', and that if we can do so, it will make us happy. I hope I can share this conviction with you.

I remember in childhood going through one of those periods we go through at that age, however good our parenting, when we feel disregarded and utterly miserable. I can't remember what this particular crisis was about: fortunately it wasn't very long-lasting, and the way it ended was this. I went out into the garden choking on tears and took a concrete path round the outside of the rose bed that lay on one side of the house. The words that were going through my mind form a time-honoured cliché, but they were 'Nobody loves me'. At the point at which the path turned back towards the cottage I heard with absolute clarity—from inside me, not outside, but just as though there *were* someone saying them—the words: 'But God loves you'.

I suppose, even after all these years, that that's the simple assumption under which I undertake this book. I believe in an underlying principle of love, whatever we want to call it and whether or not we give a name to whatever it was I meant in childhood by 'God'. I think there's plenty of good intellectual logic in philosophies which do without a god altogether, and some of them can truly help our understanding. But I do start from the principle that however we and our universe can be analysed, there is a consciousness which runs through it all, and that consciousness is a loving one. However far we feel cut off, there is something we feel cut off from, and that thing is an underlying love which is the same as life itself. Don't kid yourself that I feel this automatically, every minute of the day, in some superhuman way! But the sense of it is strong enough to make me feel that if I can't touch it at once, some sort of quietening of myself, some release of worry and distraction, will enable me to find it. A substantial amount of this book is about doing just that. What I can assure you of—and perhaps you know already from your own experience—is that when the mystical vision opens, it truly is the deepest assurance and the deepest happiness that comes, and it really does exceed by far the transient happiness that we get from outward things.

London, Summer 1997

# ACKNOWLEDGMENTS

A very supportive group of helpers has been involved in the evolution of this book from the beginning. Members of my own family read through the early draft and made many helpful suggestions, and I owe a great deal to the friends and colleagues who did the same, all of them giving generously of their time and creativity. They included Julie Burns, Michael Collishaw, Jean LeFevre, Jane Malcolmson, and Lesley Satchell. My father Geoffrey Hayward deserves special mention because of the battle he had to read it as his eyesight dimmed. It did not affect the quality of his comments. The editorial, design and production team has consisted of Annie Slocock, Kärin Baltzell and Nigel Millross; to Kärin I owe particular gratitude for the long hours she has put in at all stages without reward.

My experience has been shaped by the friends who have known me throughout my life. It really is true to say that all the people I have met have been my teacher: the ones who have put forward an opposite point of view are particularly to be thanked.

Paul Beard immediately gave permission for the quotation from his book INNER EYE, LISTENING EAR, and Pat Rodegast was also characteristically generous in allowing me to quote from EMMANUEL'S BOOK and EMMANUEL'S BOOK II.

*The wind bloweth where it listeth, and thou hearest the sound thereof, but canst not tell whence it cometh, and whither it goeth: so is every one that is born of the spirit.*

John 3 : 8

# CHAPTER ONE

# The teacher and his channel

WHEN WE speak of a teacher, we normally mean someone a little wiser than ourselves, someone who is able to impart to us particular information; and along with that information a way of working or of dealing with it. At first, the person is likely to be someone we meet through our being part of an organization like a school. Later, we may actually choose a teacher in a specific subject: singing; a personal trainer; a tai chi instructor. We select them largely on the basis of information received outwardly; perhaps a little by intuition.

We also think of our friends as our informal teachers, though wisdom even reminds us that our greatest teachers are often those who sometimes seem to be our enemies.

Another sort of teacher is the teacher we have within. The word we often use for this is intuition, and there's a helpful pun to be made on the word which makes it into in-tuition, teaching inside us.

A spiritual teacher probably combines the power that all these have to help us. How do we choose a spiritual teacher? First, I imagine that what they say will have appealed to us: it will have struck a resonant chord. I would suggest that there is more to this resonance than simply agreement. Another factor in the choice is likely to be a particularly strong intuition about the person. They will have a way of communicating to us, subtly, that they not only have deep wisdom themselves but are able to give us a perspective we lack, or believe we lack. Sometimes we may call them gurus, sages or masters, which is an acknowledgment of the enormous inner wisdom we believe they have gained through their own experience. What I would suggest is that the teacher we choose will always touch something inside us we already know, so that intuition about them and outward attraction to what they say will go hand in hand.

There is one teacher presented in this book, for it is not so much about choosing a teacher as working with one. His name is White Eagle. Exceptionally, he is not someone to whom we can ascribe precise details of birth and death; we know his voice, but the vocal chords are someone else's. Grace Cooke was White Eagle's medium, in the Spiritualist sense. She actually went into trance while he spoke, her own personality then being subordinated to his. Just what this phenomenon of trance mediumship is all about, how it works, is outside the scope of this book, but I should like from the outset to ally a message which seems to come from outside with one that comes from inside. This is because I think that someone who speaks to us through trance control is speaking mostly to our own teacher within, rather than to our mental equipment. We thus have a personal relationship with them besides the one we might have had through their medium.

When someone teaches you French, you try and remember that the verb 'to be' is *être*, and so on; but when a spiritual teacher speaks you either find that they touch something in you which makes you say 'Yes, I know that, although I've never quite thought it through', or else it doesn't do anything for you at all. The implication is that there is a body of wisdom which we know, deep within ourselves, and which a true teacher simply reawakens for us. I am not sure that this body of wisdom can ever totally be put into words, and indeed it is often the case when we respect a spiritual teacher that it isn't the literal sense of what they say that strikes us, but the sensation of familiarity with which we take it in. It may even come across to us that in it there is something very loving for us to hear: we feel as though a love comes to us, or an understanding, even if we don't catch the full sense of the words. White Eagle actually uses a phrase to describe this 'body of wisdom'. He calls it *the ancient wisdom*, something he says manifests again and again in every great spiritual teaching the world has known from the ancient Egyptians and Zoroaster to the Buddha and Jesus Christ. The name is not so important now as the implication, that in White Eagle's teaching we can afford to be open to timeless wisdom held in the collective memory. And sometimes, but not always, he will put it into words for you (the times when he does not are the times when it may be most helpful to know it for yourself, even if wordlessly).

It isn't actually clear from what I've said so far who White Eagle is and how he has managed to acquire (or uncover) the wisdom he imparts. The answer we ourselves bring to the second question may depend on our perspective. I have a feeling that if we really understood it, the way we saw his wisdom growing would not be through mental acquisition: far more of it would be through *living*, not through books. Some of it would be what he learned from his own teachers. Helpfully, White Eagle has himself described his life on earth, at least in summary, and has described this learning process, up to a point. Actually he describes several lives. His teaching presupposes that we accept not only that life continues beyond the physical level after death, but that we live many lives and acquire wisdom over a long period of time. I will return to the concept, and these lives, later.

Grace Cooke was born in 1892 and lived an ordinary kind of childhood in London in the last years of Queen Victoria. What, if anything, was different about her life from that of most children was that she had to deal, in early childhood, with the death of her mother from painful disease. She also had to cope with alienation and loneliness arising partly from this, but made worse by her father's remarriage and her being the youngest of a large family (actually the ninth child).

At this time, she began to be aware of the presence with her of what she would have called Red Indian beings, who brought her a certain courage in her situation. Among them, White Eagle made himself known to her, although he did not at first give his name; she just found him to be a loving, caring friend, much older than herself, whom she could see as clearly as she could see anyone around her, although no-one else could. From the first, he seemed to bring a glimpse of a greater dimension, too. Later, she was able to recover distinct memories of him at times when they had known one another in lives on earth, and she wrote up several of those memories for publication.

When she began (not long after) to give regular 'evidence' on the Spiritualist platform, it was generally her guide 'Lulla', a young girl, who assisted in bringing about contact between her listeners and their loved ones; but it was this older person, who by then had identified himself as White Eagle, who would offer higher advice and teaching. She began to develop a close relationship with him and he promised her that one day she would be given his picture. It was only after many years' training that it became the norm for her to go right into trance in a Spiritualist service and for him to give a full-length talk.

As I have just said, Grace Cooke wrote on a number of occasions about her relationship with her guide. PLUMED SERPENT, which was published in 1942, outlines one of the reincarnational memories just mentioned. Another of her books which was partly past-life and partly present-life memory was THE SHINING PRESENCE (1946). In the following passage from that book, she explains how White Eagle had two levels on which he communicated with her, one familiar and personal, the other much more at the level of the higher teacher.

*In my childhood I had often seen Indians round my bed and had become quite familiar with their appearance, especially one who called himself 'White Eagle', but I had not hitherto seen any of them in their higher spiritual aspect. 'The Shining Presence' came to me robed in pure white, his cloak gathered at the throat with a great clasp of amethyst and attached also at the wrists, so that when he raised his hands in blessing it gave the appearance of wings, snow-white and beautiful. On his head he wore a crown of white plumed feathers. At first glance it gave the impression of a North American Chief's war bonnet, but when I better understood the symbolism it revealed him as an initiate—a Plumed Serpent. He seemed to emerge or take form from a cloud or mist of soft white light. As he gradually became more distinct his robes scintillated so that they appeared to be covered with countless gems dazzling and wonderful.*

*I did not always see him; sometimes I heard his message only. When this happened my spirit was usually attuned or exalted so that I could meet him, as it were, half way. Quite often I heard his voice speaking, rich and musical. In simple language he would teach me spiritual truths; tell me of things that were to come and how I was to make preparation.* *

---

*THE SHINING PRESENCE, p. 20. The reincarnational memories in the two books mentioned are today available together in the book THE ILLUMINED ONES (for details of this and all books mentioned in the text, see the reading plan below, pp.166ff).

In his teaching White Eagle often speaks of a higher self and a lower self, the latter being the one that is most recognizable in the everyday personality. Here, undoubtedly, we have White Eagle in his higher aspect, but maybe with a hint of something more. Often people try to ascribe to White Eagle the status of a 'master', but this account by his medium is probably the closest he or she ever came to using that sort of word. Modesty at all times was and is his watchword, and I think he would prefer to point to the master in all of us: something more realized in some than in others, but in all of us it is there not only as potential, but as something which only has to be inwardly recognized.

It is therefore useful to read another account, written by Grace Cooke's husband Ivan for the White Eagle magazine *Angelus* (June 1938, pp. 193–94), in which we are much more in touch with the humanness of White Eagle's personality as it came across to his listeners. In the opening paragraph I think it is the particular conditions of a private interview with White Eagle that is being recalled; such interviews were not uncommon in those days.

*White Eagle, you learn from him, is only a simple soul, and lays no claim to profound knowledge or omniscience; he defers to your opinion, submits to your judgment, lays the responsibility of decision on* you. *True, from his standpoint he sees that this or that may happen, that this or that course would be the wiser; but the choice must be yours, and it is for you to follow the pointing finger or ignore it.*

*He is simple and gentle; yet with a simplicity that is the essence of all profundity; and to that which is simple and sweet within humanity he appeals. According to the measure of truth within ourselves, so is our welcome and response, and to the critical, the overweeningly intellectual, he has no message other than a patience and a forbearance which often reaches to and wins its own response despite those intolerances.*

*He sees within, how deeply he and God alone know; and sees, wonderfully enough in each of us, something redemptive, good, pure and indeed Christlike. The baser he does not see; in all the years we have known him he has never condemned, never criticized any one man or woman, never shown himself irritated, disappointed or heartsick; yet the waywardness of those he strives to help, their misinterpretation of his message, their capacity to seize on the one item which fits their own desires and forgetfulness of others, would break many a mortal heart.*

Somewhere between these two ways of regarding White Eagle, the one exalted and the other human, might be put the watercolour painting of him which eventually came to his medium just as he had promised, and in which she immediately recognized him. It had been painted twenty years previously, but the artist had felt inspired not to part with it, and said that he had known that in due course he would be led to the person for whom it was intended. It is available in a colour reproduction with the following explanation.

*The artist in time came to her as a total stranger, introduced casually through a friend, and at the sitting White Eagle told this man that he had years previously painted the heads of two American Indians: one full face, and the other in profile with a headdress of eagle's feathers, white with blue and gold tips; and that the latter was his portrait.*

Needless to say, the portrait was as White Eagle described (technically it was in three-quarters, rather than in profile, but I put this discrepancy down to the constant retelling of the story). The artist, R. Vicaji, was delighted to present the painting to White Eagle's medium.

One of the questions I have been asked, particularly on visits to the United States, is why does the painting show White Eagle with blue eyes? Almost universally, Native Americans have brown eyes, and the choice of blue is therefore remarkable. It is a curious point. The painting had been done many years before by an artist with enough knowledge to draw a Native American in an authentic way: why should he apparently get so important a detail wrong? None of us will ever know for sure. I feel a significance in it myself, however, and it relates to the higher and the lower aspects of the personality, just touched upon. White Eagle was not *just* a Native American; the blue eyes give a sense of timeless wisdom, of deep mystical vision, and it is one of the things that authenticates the portrait for me, not the reverse. Focus on his eyes only, and you may see in them a hint of the Chinese teacher; if you examine the details of the face, you may acquire insights into his other lives as well. Truly the artist must have seen a most complex personality; and with extraordinary precision, I think, he brought it into the picture.

The relationship between White Eagle and his medium, Grace Cooke, is central to much of what we read in his teaching. Among her memories were two of being White Eagle's daughter, one in an Egyptian and one in an Andean life. From these incarnations she recalled the name Minesta, one which I shall use in this book because she was so generally known by it during her later life. An other name by which White Eagle sometimes referred to her is also eloquent, though: it was 'Brighteyes'. She seems to have been carefully trained so that she could act as a clear channel (that is to say, so that she could receive impressions and words from him through her psychic faculty but at the heart level, without excessive interference from her own mind). Though the mind needed to be subdued, one imagines that her own vocabulary needed somewhat to be developed to enable White Eagle to find adequate words; although he himself said that the characteristic she had most needed to develop to channel him was simplicity.

She was not the sort of medium who takes down scripts blindly in another language and character system than their own, but one whose own language intermingled well with his. Even then, there were occasions when White Eagle acknowledged that there were simply not the words available to express what he wanted to say. She could never hear what he said when he spoke publicly, but she was herself absolutely imbued with his teaching. On occasions when not acting as his medium, she could speak inspirationally, somewhat overshadowed by White Eagle but presenting her own personality to her audience.

Ivan Cooke refers, in the pair of articles from which I have just made quotation, to three things which have to be developed in such a person. One is the psychic faculty; the next is the character, so that the weaknesses of a physical life do not mar the gift; and the third is the verbal command which enables the guide sufficiently to express himself or herself. Such an expectation 'obviously makes no small demand on the capacity of the guide's instrument', he says.

Minesta's early work, as I stated, was largely clairvoyance: looking at people's individual lives and circumstances with clear vision and thus providing help. She did this, and gave evidence of survival, for a full twelve years before ever White Eagle gave his first public address. As his opportunity to communicate increased, White Eagle sought through his medium to teach everyone how to open their own eyes to the world of spirit and, later, how to do this through meditation. As a result, people's individual contact with White Eagle, independent of Minesta's mediumship, grew. He became a group teacher, not the guide of one individual, although throughout her lifetime Minesta remained his mouthpiece, and the 'Mother' of the Lodge continues to be the sympathetic mouthpiece of the teacher today.

Perhaps I could explain that term 'Mother'. It is roughly what the name 'Minesta' means. It feels as though White Eagle is (from spirit) the chief of the tribe, or at the least its 'wise man'. However, this role is complemented at the earthly level by a feminine aspect, the 'Mother'. It is to her that the job of hearing and interpreting is given, and in her clarity of vision and inspired speaking the presence of White Eagle is often to be witnessed.

As Minesta's grandson, I might add that the sense of her being a mother was also most warmly evident to us all at the very personal level. She took a huge interest in her family, was always generous with treats, loved to see us grandchildren grow up and go through school and university, took us away on holidays, and so on. The life she had missed out on in her own childhood was not going to be forfeited by any of us if she could help it. She was very human, too: far from perfect, lots of things in her wounded childhood remaining evident; and yet to use a phrase from a recent book title, if ever there was a *good enough* mother and grandmother, I am sure it was she.

White Eagle is now felt as a real companion by an increasingly large number of people. Yet it is not within the framework of what we understand about him that he would publicly use another as a specific channel to address a new audience. He has made it clear that our work in these days is to open up our own inner wisdom to hear him, and to use another would seem to frustrate this design. When he speaks in the Lodge, he offers his own unmistakeable identity.

## Partnership

One reason for my bringing the medium so firmly into the picture is that her life demonstrates what happens when one lives out his teaching with total commitment and this book is about integrity of teaching and practice. When I write of my grandmother, though, it is inevitable that personal memories and memories of her public work are intermingled. One of the things I most remember her for is her unwavering conviction and sense of purpose. She almost never doubted her real work, and she could therefore put her belief about the reality of spirit into words with absolute authenticity. If she felt that her words could be helpful to someone, she never missed the opportunity to write a little note of comfort, or loving support when they were 'down'. Often this relied entirely on her clairvoyance; no-one, using earthly communication, had told her that this or that friend needed help; very often no-one knew. But *she* did, and I know that one of the things she was so much loved for was precisely this aspect of her nature. It seems to me one of the best uses one can make of psychic powers.

The other point about her was that in her unshakeable conviction she always, and often against weighty material advice, followed the voice of spirit guidance. When White Eagle gave the instruction in 1945, towards the end of the war, that a country centre for the work must be chosen, she set out and found it. Although she had no funds to count on, New Lands was bought at the same time as the commitment was made to purchase the freehold of the Lodge's London premises. Today, the purchase of either would be unthinkable, at current prices and on the Lodge's funding level. This is but one of many examples. White Eagle really *was* her teacher, and if he guided her in a particular way, she acted unquestioningly. Although I would counsel that everyone (to use St John's phrase) *Try the spirits, whether they are of God,*\* nevertheless it is one of my aims in this book to promote such a trust of the spirit, this fidelity to the inner wisdom as against the prevailing opinion of the world.

Minesta's vision applied to far more than material things. The very titles PLUMED SERPENT, THE SHINING PRESENCE and THE ILLUMINED

\*1 John 4 : 1.

ONES (a combined volume of the memories in the other two), imply a recognition of the quality of life demonstrated by the people among whom she spent her previous lives. The sense that one could be 'illumined'—that the inner light, which she believed represented God within, might shine radiantly outwards—was something she felt intensely. She believed that the human being could ultimately, in this way, be transformed.

White Eagle speaks of this level of life in a talk that was published in another early edition of White Eagle's magazine. In the course of recalling a memory of his Native American lifetimes he also describes a conscious way to see with the 'inner eye'.

*In one of my incarnations I lived much among the pine trees ... trees so tall, so straight, so self-reliant. They sway in the breeze, but remain upright like sentinels. They welcome the dawn; they bless the setting sun; they make music with the swaying of their foliage; they give out such fragrance. They are full of magical fire. If you want to see this fire of nature, go to the pines and, putting your back against a pine tree, look from this eye within the brain [White Eagle indicated the pineal gland] in shape like a pine cone. See the light, the little fires which glow at the bottom of the tree trunk, and call to your angelic friends, to the spirits of the air, to come, and then see the effect!...*

*We did not [then] know death as you know death today. There was no separation between any one of you and your beloved one when the outer covering was laid aside. Life was one beautiful and grand harmony, but we did not need earthly possessions. We did not know worldly civilization; and this is a path of training you will also learn to dispense with.*

*Angelus*, vol. 4 (1940), p. 84

Those parting words, which I think will probably seem rather remarkable to most ears, will echo in the last chapter, when I take up White Eagle's teaching about how, eventually, we actually overcome death.

Life after death; the overcoming of death: two different concepts. What links them in White Eagle's teaching is the sense that spirit life is real, earth life a rather insistent illusion. Our conditioning about death imprisons us, White Eagle would say. In this book I should like to be able to demonstrate that if we live with full awareness every minute of our lives we already live in a world way beyond the confines of physical mortality.

## 'The Lodge' as framework for the teaching

So what is the character of this 'Lodge' that has been built around the experience of working with White Eagle's teaching? It arises, first, out of White Eagle's own precept that we learn through interaction with others better than in isolation. The Lodge is a place where people are able to explore this. It goes without saying that one can benefit from his teaching without any involvement in the Lodge and indeed follow a personal path, paying attention first to the teacher within and then to White Eagle as one of a number of teachers. Yet White Eagle actually advocates a one-pointed approach for the sheer efficiency of doing so.

The Lodge might be called a family or a community, but it is not a residential community. The connections people feel are more inward ones than structured ones. However, it functions as an organization through branches ('Daughter Lodges') and small groups which hold meetings, often with opportunities for meditation and retreat. As a community, its keynote is service and in this the service of healing is central.

Beyond this the Lodge rather happily resists definition. It is always more than an 'organization', for at heart it is a family in which all are equal and as one. It can possibly be described as a

church, because there is a ritual to its work in the shape of services both of worship and of healing which is adhered to, in its
basic form, all over the world. Yet it is not a church in the sense
of having a defined set of dogmas, however much there may be a
sense of shared belief such as is amplified in this book. In America
the word 'church' is used more often to describe it than in Europe; and when I turn back to the first page of the very first issue
of *Angelus* in 1936 the term is used there too, though anything
but exclusively.

*The White Eagle Lodge holds no creed save unity with all, no
other aim save brotherhood. The name chosen for the Lodge is
designed not for the enhancement of any one individual, in-
carnate or discarnate, but as representative of a school or aspect of thought which might be symbolized by the white eagle—the bird of vision, of soaring wings and sunlit skies. In
this connection it may be well to recall that the symbol of an
eagle has always represented the mystical aspect of Christianity as embodied in the fourth gospel, of St John.*

*If it be loyal to itself, the Lodge should seek to be a mysti-
cal church of the spirit, its mission to send forth such truth as
has been entrusted to it; to hold nothing to itself, but ever seek
to give; to place service before numbers, power, or popularity
in a world where service is desperately needed. Such a church
is fulfilling itself if some who are lonely can find in it compan-
ionship and affection; if some who have lost faith can find a
stable resting place again; and if the sick in mind or body can
gain from its healing the health of soul and body they lack.*

Ivan Cooke's words indicate his own clear commitment to a
church of broad open vision. Virtually all of this would stand
today, except that there is an unintentional hint in this passage
of a strong axis between need and giving. Today, I should prefer
to feel that everyone was first and foremost able to express their

inner truth in the sanctuary of the Lodge; that they grew through being there, whatever path or desire led them.

I think my grandfather's vision here is as powerfully influenced by the symbol of a lighthouse as by any conventional idea of 'church'. Ultimately, I personally believe the word 'Lodge' is still the most helpful. Although for many it may offer connotations of a masonic lodge, the sense intended is that of a Native American communal dwelling or meeting place. It is a 'shared roof' for a particular tribe. This is certainly the sense I should like to offer in this book. Any masonic sense there might be comes from a feeling for an inner wisdom among White Eagle's students, wisdom that is secret because sacred, but actually no more than the sharing, at an inner level, of the simplest truths of the heart—the same as the 'ancient wisdom' mentioned earlier. At the Lodge's centre there is an inner brother–sisterhood of souls who hold the vision and ensure its continuity; at its widest, it provides a place where those who wish to find their inner truth may find encouragement, refreshment and healing.

The vision at the heart of the work is that spirit is our reality, not matter. Although his request is not that his followers should proselytize, it is clear that White Eagle's purpose is that they should help humanity to find a vision that makes life more fulfilling, more radiant. Above all, to help them be happy. I referred earlier to 'the White Eagle work', but it is never work with a heavy sense of purpose. This work is done quietly, partly through self-realization and partly by a conscious use of inner gifts which include the projection of the healing light or Christ light into the world. By Christ light (a term White Eagle uses often) is meant something embodied by Jesus of Nazareth, but not something tied uniquely to Jesus as an individual: rather, something which comes from within all of us and is of unconquerable power. This light is symbolized by the six-pointed Star (a symbol to be described shortly). This is a Christ symbol, rather than a Christian symbol, in that it represents a quality or essence, not a teaching.

## More about White Eagle

A little more remains to be said of the teacher himself in the context of this chapter. To me he is one who, surprisingly, since he is not in a physical body, gives a sense of being a very warm, balanced, *human* soul. Above all he shows great love for all human beings and deep respect for them as they walk their pathway, wherever that may lead them. He does not judge, for, as he often says, he has trodden the road of incarnation himself and knows how arduous its challenges can be. White Eagle is aware that the blindness souls take on in order to fit themselves into a human frame disposes them to all sorts of fears and troubled emotions—and so to ill-health. Most frequently he speaks of himself as simply the spokesman for a brotherhood in the world of light who seek to help humanity through guidance and loving watchfulness. Yet he is also very much to be felt as a personality, one who matches wisdom with kindly humour.

White Eagle tells us only a little of the specific historical existence in which he acquired the name by which he is known. He gives hints of his life as a Mohawk at the time of the Iroquois Federation, which was a turning-point in Native American history and an inspiration when some of the democratic ideals of the United States Constitution, unchanged today, were framed. It is pleasing that the essential harmony between White Eagle's teachings and the traditions of the Native Americans has been verified in recent years through personal connections members have made with the native peoples. This harmony comes across in his teaching about the importance of the natural world, and about the thinness of the veil which divides this world and the spirit life. The wise 'Indian' of both past and present would emphasize as White Eagle does that it is spirit that is the primary level; and would, I think, teach us to see right through the obscurity of matter. Out of many quotations one might choose from today's Native Americans, the following, entitled 'How to talk to God', seems to me to be absolutely in the spirit of this book. I'm not sure that so rigorous a discipline as is asked for here is necessary in the West, but I love the directness of it.

*When we want wisdom we go up on the hill and talk to God. Four days and four nights, without food and water. Yes, you can talk to God up on a hill by yourself. You can say anything you want. Nobody's there to listen to you. That's between you and God and nobody else. It's a great feeling to be talking to God. I know. I did it way up on the mountain. The wind was blowing. It was dark. It was cold. And I stood there and I talked to God.* \*

Directness is often a splendid quality. One of the passages in White Eagle's teaching about himself that I particularly value was given in an early message. I like it because it so well emphasizes that he is made of the same stuff as we are.

*Who are we who bring you this message? With what authority do we speak? We are spiritual beings, even as you are also spirit—you manifest through the flesh, we are of the unseen, yet lent the power to make ourselves manifest and audible to you. What is my nationality? I have none! You may go to your wardrobe and select the dress or clothes thought suitable to some particular occasion. I also; for in my 'wardrobe' there hangs the raiment—the personality, the mentality, the nationality—which I have worn during*

*The words of Mathew King, from WISDOMKEEPERS by Steve Wall and Harvey Arden, p. 31.

*my past lives or incarnations. One of these I don, accord-ing to the occasion, and therefore I may return as a North American Indian, an Englishman, a Tibetan, an Egyptian; but always it is the same spirit speaking, a spirit which has passed through many experiences. If what I have to say has any worth it is only because of the wider experience which has been mine....*

Angelus, vol. 4 (1940), pp. 94–95

The Native American figure of the white eagle means a wise teacher, a connection made because it is said that of all the birds it is the only one that can fly directly towards the sun. Thus it is the one that has the clearest vision of the place which we all strive to reach. Moreover, by showing us the technique of flight the eagle shows us how we may attain the vision. I would sug-gest that eyes of the spirit are not only what White Eagle has, but also what he would most like us to be able to share.

As the very notion of a discarnate being, one without a body, may not be easily accepted unless the reader has a prior disposi-tion to do so, I would suggest that it is as well to let the bounda-ries of our own culture go into the background a little and re-member how natural that belief is in other cultures. Thus, the eloquent words of Chief Seattle, most often quoted of all Native Americans, contain the promise that those of his race who have perished will always walk the continent:

*Our dead never forget the beautiful world that gave them be-ing. They still love its winding rivers, its great mountains and its sequestered vales, and they ever yearn in tenderest affec-tion over the lonely hearted living and often return to visit and comfort them.* *

No modern rigidity of thought restrains the seventh-century Christian writer Adamnan, either, who wrote an account of St

*Spoken by Chief Seattle or Seathl in 1854 and recorded by Dr Henry Smith. In HOW CAN ONE SELL THE AIR?, Summertown, Tennessee, 1992.

Columba (founder of the Celtic church in dark-age Britain) in which he speaks easily of Columba's powers of prescience, out-of-the-body travel, performing of miracles, and fellowship with angels. You will find that it is in the spirit of this book that some statements are better taken in imaginative trust, and not analysed too hard or defined. When I make this demand of the reader it is deliberate; I do not decry the mind, but regard it as being at its most useful when it is in the service of the higher wisdom which the 'heart' offers, not vice versa.

## A personality of many facets

The personality that is felt from White Eagle, as the passage quoted earlier (p. 29) shows, is more complex than one linked entirely to a single life in North America. He tells us elsewhere how he grew up and eventually served as a teacher among Egyptian, Andean and other peoples. One may also recognize in his talks (just as in his portrait) an old Chinese teacher, and more than a hint of the Buddhist. The latter influence shows not only in the symbols he gives us for use in meditation and in his teaching about the nature of the soul, but also in an emphasis on mindfulness, attentiveness. A favourite passage that comes to mind is one in which he asks that when you are speaking to someone, give them the courtesy of your absolute attention (Buddhism blended with a Christian moral respect!); or if hammering a nail into a piece of wood, that you concentrate upon it with your whole being. No one of these influences is paramount. At times he feels more of a Francis of Assisi in character, deeply human yet with an absolutely driving conviction. His character has much of the sweetness of Columba, who sometimes feels very close to him too (both figures, it might be added, were pretty robust as well as gentle!). But anyone reading his exposition of the gospel of St John will recognize immediately the aptness of Ivan Cooke's words (quoted on p. 26) about the connection between White Eagle's name and the symbol of the evangelist.*

While those who read some of the writings of the Essenes (a community which began just before the Christian era) may point out similarities with White Eagle's teaching, his 'Christianity' has a Gnostic feel to it too: the belief that truth lies in inner knowledge and can be found there through reflection, and work on and with the self. 'Gnosis' means knowledge and the Gnostics were the original rival to the orthodox teachers in the interpretation of Christian teaching. Many White Eagle students also feel a link with the Cathars, part-heir to this tradition (the Cathars or Albigenses were a sect who flourished in parts of Europe, particularly in southern France, in the early middle ages and were largely exterminated by crusades by the Catholic church in the thirteenth century). I say this carefully because comparison with another teaching often brings up unwanted associations which confuse. Thus, the Cathars' very severe separation of spirit and matter is beautifully softened, to say the least, in White Eagle's teaching. He says that the earth is *full* of spirit where the Cathars regarded it as being alien to spirit.

Gnostic teachings take many forms, and where White Eagle's vision is most akin to them is in its freshness, its feeling that spirit is real and alive. I would not want to appropriate William Blake either to Gnosticism or to White Eagle's teaching, and yet the closest I can get to a visual representation of White Eagle's 'eyes of the spirit' vision would still be some of those wonderful visionary watercolours of Blake's. Actually, everyone has their own form in which they conceive of spirit. Words from me could

---

*For the reference to hammering the nail, see THE GENTLE BROTHER, p. 62, and for the symbol of the evangelist, see THE LIVING WORD OF ST JOHN.

easily narrow that vision. Yet *freshness* is a word I would hold to, and hope it would recur for each reader as he or she comes upon the various White Eagle quotations in this book.

Some doctrinal issues are unavoidable, even if in discussing them I soften them by seeking to give the spirit, not the letter, of White Eagle's teaching. For instance, it should be said that the time-span given for the soul's perfection both in Gnosticism and in White Eagle is a long one. White Eagle's teaching is generous in its scope and he frequently asserted that it is not vital to hold to a doctrine like reincarnation (although he does, with a twinkling eye, suggest that it is most irrational not to!). The concept of a 'vital' belief is indeed alien to his teaching: everyone is on the road to 'salvation', he would say, simply by the growing realization of the light within their heart and not by their adopting particular beliefs.

White Eagle is not a teacher who offers instant fixes or one who takes from his students responsibility for their own lives. He often seems to be a better guide to take us through the discoveries that men and women have already made about their purpose for being, than one who overturns the thought of others. If we take him as a teacher we still have to do a great deal of work ourselves! Yet there is something revolutionary about his teaching too, a hint *always* that enlightenment can be found at any moment, not just at the end of a long road. I hope that the succeeding chapters will help to reveal this.

# CHAPTER TWO

# The experience of working with a spiritual teacher

IT IS VERY common to find people disenchanted with the idea of a priest or minister standing as interpreter between them and God. Then, having abandoned orthodox religion, many choose to go it alone, and to take no-one as their guide except themselves. This is a courageous path, but I do not necessarily think it is one we have to adopt in giving up the idea of the priest. It can be deeply helpful, reassuring in a way that is normally very positive, to have a chosen guide, so long as we do not allow our relationship to a teacher to turn into one of dependency. What White Eagle offers, I believe, is an example of how to internalize God, to find the divine being within ourselves, while allowing scope for communal experience and shared worship.

He would himself begin by saying that there is no *real* guide except the guide in one's heart. In chapter one I emphasized the closeness White Eagle's teaching may have to what we feel within. I said, you may remember, that wisdom is something we have deep within ourselves, and a true teacher simply reawakens it for us. But that is precisely why a teacher is useful: it is often much easier to have someone outside ourselves who prompts us. A teacher's experience saves us time, both on account of their better perspective and the attention to detail they have learnt. I know when I have had individual lessons on some practical subject I have been most helped by the sort of teacher who notices everything and carries on with infinite patience, pointing out every little thing that needs working on. In White Eagle's teaching we go on discovering these promptings inwardly, by reading or hearing his words. The training goes on just as long as we permit ourselves to be guided.

The real teacher thus brings out our buried understanding. The old Zen masters who set their pupils *koans* or enigmatic questions were only seeking to awaken forgotten awareness. The true teacher does not beguile us with his or her erudition or seduce us with promises, though he or she does take us further in understanding than we *thought* we knew.

The experience of being aware that White Eagle is sufficiently close for us to draw upon his wisdom and to feel comfort from his love, is something many, many people have shared. I know that when I have faced a big ordeal, White Eagle's presence has been all the more real for me. The understanding in his eyes has soothed me many times when I have felt upset with myself, or inspired me to deeper understanding when I was seeing things shallowly. Once I recall driving out of London, very much behind schedule, and getting the clearest possible sensation not only that my intuitive guidance would give me better route-directions than my mind (and it did!) but also that I was running, slightly off the ground, with White Eagle alongside: both of us in youth, fleet of foot. At other times I have been strongly aware of him not as North American, but South, bringing the solar power of Andean civilization; and once in a similar form, but almost more as a pillar of light than as an ordinary being.

Something that demonstrates for me (perhaps incongruously at first) how White Eagle is an internal as well as an external teacher is the common experience when his teaching is being heard (when one of his talks is read in a service or even when a tape is being played or a book read quietly), that he is present *now*. I am very used to studying, in a scholarly way, the teachings of the past and yet no-one I read comes alive for me in the way White Eagle does. When he spoke during Minesta's lifetime he spoke slowly and from what seemed like a place deep within her (the most noticeable variation from her ordinary voice was that it was deeper and resonated more). I remember how, in a public service, her actual countenance would change during the moments beforehand; and when she rose from her seat it would be in a way that, although she reached forward for something firm to hold onto, was very much the rising of someone stronger, and manifestly other, than herself. Sometimes there was just a hint of yet another overshadowing *him*: giving credence to what he has always maintained, that he is simply a spokesman for a still higher being or group.

Although White Eagle's meaning was never difficult to follow during a trance address, sometimes—for we are all human, and this was my own childhood and early life—I remember how easy it was to dismiss what he was saying. The words came slowly, and so differently from hearing a lecture, or a speaker on radio or television. Then, just as I least expected it, I would hear something with such force that it dramatically opened whole new areas of understanding for me. People would say how such an experience could utterly open the heart and leave you in a different state entirely from how you were before. Something I remember happening quite frequently (and still do find happening with White Eagle's teaching when it is read in a service today) was that afterwards people would insist that what White Eagle had said which most had helped them was such and such. Yet to the next person, and again to myself, what he had said was something quite different: what *each* of us needed to hear—a shared experience but a different message in each case!

I think this demonstrates that what White Eagle does is gently to lull the outer mind and then, largely through loving intelligence, imperceptibly to raise the hearer's consciousness. Then what is heard or read is not necessarily the literal sense. We may read between the lines, or we may hear our own truth, prompted by the words themselves (which I think more exactly describes the experience); or we may hear a message that White Eagle is conveying to us at a subtler level than that of mere words.

Such a means of communicating with us is very special. Merely to go to White Eagle for a precise answer on something is not the best way of using his teaching (even though I know of many individuals who in a 'sitting' with him in the early days received very detailed information). Were you to look up all the references to the idea of karma, for instance, in his published teaching, you might just end up muddled if you tried to take them all at their face value. For just such a reason I go on to include a discussion of what he calls the law of karma in chapter five of this book. Yet I am pretty certain that at least one of the references would have struck you with particular force, taken you up beyond the confines of intellectual debate ('into the temple of wisdom', White Eagle might say), and illumined your understanding for a moment. It rarely pays to come to White Eagle with too literal a mind, and although he is not as obviously wily as some of the Zen teachers were in their methods, he does have a good reason for the subtlety or otherwise of everything he says.

It would be an unhelpful teacher indeed who defined everything for us, nor would it pay to seek this. No true teacher would diminish our own power to develop understanding. Definition in spiritual matters is generally limitation (White Eagle would aver), because only the heart can comprehend infinity, and love, the principle behind all things, is itself infinite. Arguments could go on for ever if one person took a statement White Eagle had made and set it against a passage chosen by another, both parties insisting on the literal sense. One of them might claim a more up-to-the-minute reference than the other, but as he says, 'There is no new truth'.* Whenever a subject is discussed, there is always the possibility that the circumstances of the occasion—the needs of the listeners present or the demands of their strong minds—led him to speak in a particular way, thus giving the message a different bias; or even that the medium's own mind filtered his words somehow.

Any medium does this, I might say: what I think was special about Minesta was how much it stood out that her working relationship with White Eagle arose out of long association and that she had a real gift of putting her own mind to one side. I do not know of any medium whose teaching was *less* influenced by what she herself thought and felt. I think it also true to say that White Eagle as a teacher is multidimensional in the way he works. As Paul Beard points out in his book INNER EYE, LISTENING EAR (p. 137), in White Eagle there is 'both a personal and an impersonal pointing of the way'. He mentions how Minesta

*was well aware of a deeper White Eagle who lay behind the wise, gentle, humorous White Eagle his pupils knew so well. This deeper White Eagle, though equally loving, was more stern. 'We do not flatter', he once said, 'our love for you is pure'.*

It is always worth remembering White Eagle's desire to lift the consciousness of his hearer to their own higher understanding. Sometimes this is done softly, humorously, and sometimes with

*From *Stella Polaris*, vol. 4 (1955), p. 14.

greater solemnity (I would prefer that word to sternness). Words I quoted in chapter one ('We are spiritual beings, even as you are also spirit') emphasize how important for him is the source of what he says, how relatively unimportant the guise in which the words come. I think the need to hear the spirit behind the words, not the literal meaning, is something almost forced upon us by his not being too present, and this is one of the joys of having a true *spiritual* teacher, not an earthly one. Could any other sort of teacher convince us that we are spirit?

## Putting the teaching into practice

It would not be unfair to object that if White Eagle was always one remove away—speaking through a medium—and if the medium herself is now 'in the next world' as we casually put it, it might be better to choose a teacher who is more present in the conventional sense. I think what I have already said is one answer to this. The very fact that White Eagle is discarnate and we have to make some of the effort, helps to draw us up—lift our consciousness—to a higher level. A large number of the people who come to White Eagle's teaching feel in some way drawn to it at a level beyond the intellectual, so the objection does not wholly apply for them; but it is not one that I would shrink from dealing with. I think there is less danger of dependency, more demand of our own creativity, in such a teacher.

In adolescence, striving as we all tend to against the constraints which family traditions imposed upon me, I was rather inclined to think that White Eagle's teaching functioned perfectly well on its own without a 'Lodge' to contain it, and I felt that the teaching would long outlast the shell into which it was being put. Now I rather feel that it is not a shell at all, but that the Lodge is in fact a space where we try out living life in a way that is illuminated by White Eagle's teaching. It is this continuing experiment that makes White Eagle's teaching a living teaching, not a completed one. If the Lodge is what the teaching tends to be clad in, then it feels more like a loose skin than an external skeleton around the teaching. So often White Eagle says that he would sooner leave to us the way we put into practice what he says: he gives us a lead, and respects us enough to imply 'you will know better than we how to do this in your own life'.

In another context he says: 'Give way on little things that don't matter, but on matters of principle stand firm as a rock'. It is indeed an instruction given many times.* I think that similarly he gives us principles, and leaves it as part of our training to interpret them, to separate the matters of detail from the issues of principle, and to recognize whether in the way we act we really have done as we would have liked to do, or let ourselves down. The Lodge is designed for us and by us (and by our subtle guides) as a way of our working out our lessons and expressing our creativity, and who knows where that may take us?

To the extent that this book is interpretation, I hope it will be superseded in the same way as it perhaps supersedes others that have gone before. The character of the Lodge itself is an interpretation of the teaching. That means—and I really hope this is so—that the opportunities for it to take on a rigid structure are actually limited; it means it has to change every time that the way we wish to experiment with living the teaching changes. Sometimes this needs clearly noticing so that it is acted upon at the right time. The value of a discarnate teacher is that our understanding of what they say has constantly to be re-evaluated, because we go on hearing their words within, as well as without.

Once upon a time most of White Eagle's followers were drawn from the Spiritualist movement in Britain and (in a small way)

*e.g. in SPIRITUAL UNFOLDMENT 4, p. 102.

40

abroad. The services derived from Spiritualism to the extent that they included an element of traditional clairvoyance. At the outset Minesta transmitted White Eagle's response to people's individual concerns, as they appeared from spirit, and he brought them in touch with loved ones who were missed and grieved over. With the development of meditation teaching and White Eagle's greater emphasis on communion rather than communication in the psychic sense, this element was eventually dropped. Thus the Lodge changed. People were instead encouraged to make their own contact with those they had 'lost', through a period of meditational communion in the service. There was, and indeed still is, a quiet period in the service set aside for this. This way, White Eagle said, we were more likely to reach the celestial (the highest) plane of thought than what he called the higher astral (in general, the plane contacted by psychics).

In the 1970s, I recall a deeply inspired address in which my aunt, Joan Hodgson, spoke of a new task. The time was coming for a degree of withdrawal in the very demonstrable help we received through Minesta. White Eagle's medium was then undoubtedly approaching her own passing and Joan made it clear that henceforth the task was to build for ourselves the very 'bridge of light' to our spirit teachers that had formerly been conspicuously maintained for us by Minesta. Since then I believe we have all been the more keen to hear and feel the presence of White Eagle with and around us—and that of Minesta too.

In such ways, the Lodge moves on and grows, and as the world itself changes the Lodge acquires new tasks. When it began, one of the beliefs already in force was that its members should assist humanity in overcoming 'the mad fear of death'. With the outbreak of war imminent, that felt all-important. Then, under White Eagle's guidance, during the second world war, the Lodge undertook an enormous task to work at an inner level upon the attitudes and minds of men and women in order to help free them from fear. Since then we have found, I think, that this phrase, 'the mad fear of death', is not only linked to violent death (maybe this was always true). The fear of death is something which to a greater or lesser extent keeps every one of us locked in a level of realization way below our potential. It is as much a fear about existence as a fear of the loss of existence. To release ourselves and others from that is every bit as real a task as helping to overcome the fear of death by enemy action. As Milton said, 'Peace hath her victories no less renowned than war'.

Since 1945, the threat of annihilation has tended to focus on the power of nuclear weapons; but up to a point humanity has recovered its own, redeeming, self-control on this point and the threat has become less real. When the individual reasserts his or her own inner power not only do the fears tend to go, but the causes of fear with them. In the new climate, people's fears focus more particularly upon problems within society: higher levels of violence, increasing portrayal of violence in the electronic media, the threat to the environment, family breakdowns, distrust of institutions, drug abuse and the emergence of new and apparently untreatable diseases. I believe we can overcome these fears too through developing awareness.

White Eagle is always comforting when our fears are to the fore. True, he reminds us that we are at the cusp of a new age symbolized by a new zodiacal sign, Aquarius, and that the transition is bound to produce major changes as old traditions and systems give way to new ones. However, he sets his students a charge to help humanity overcome their fears, just as much today as in 1938, or 1940, or 1962, or whatever date we might compare. White Eagle applies the term 'the years of fire' to all the present period, including the last war. Some people relate these years to what are described as 'earth changes'. While he has never ruled out that the times ahead may be difficult, the theme of continuity is far more important in his teaching than anything to do with cataclysm. Even during the war years this was the way he described the transition to the new age: 'We see the old order, even the old presentation of religion, changing. We do not foresee violent upheavals, but this gradual permeation of human kind by the spirit.'*

The current process of distrust of all our institutions is far more in line with his predictions than are catastrophic earthquakes or natural disasters. Threats of irreversible ecological imbalance and collapse are part of today's media vocabulary, but White Eagle gives much more of a sense that these dangers have a purpose which is to bring new attitudes out of humanity, rather than that they are potentially final. I think he would say that humanity's gradual discovery of its responsibility to the planet is precisely what the divine plan entails. This is why the threats to the planet are allowed in the first place. In this way he restores a sense of deep design and purpose when he considers any issue.

What a model White Eagle sets us, if from the spiritual perspective all things have their purpose and nothing is random! He goes further, though, and reminds us that we have the power to affect our future in much greater ways than material science deems possible. In the chapters that follow I shall discuss his teaching about how we can positively use the power of the light to bring about change and healing. An organization bearing his name has the challenge to respond not only with inner spiritual work, but also to be an accepting and loving place for those who come to it with very real wounds, from childhood or from later life-circumstances. As I said, the Lodge has been designed for growth and education, not just for healing!

*Angelus, October 1943, p. 11.

Of course the difficulties start when it becomes clear that it is designed for *everyone's* growth, not just ours personally, whether we are newcomers or have been involved for many years! Personalities are not normally designed to be easy: they are like rough stone, to be worn smooth. So, often, the Lodge is a place where people work out their life issues in the active sense, as well as one where they find refuge and healing away from some of life's most trying demands. Within its centres the Lodge does try to provide truly 'safe' spaces—perhaps also within a counselling situation—where feelings can be expressed without infringing on other people's space. Nonetheless, the emotions are unpredictable, and of course they break through at times which seem inappropriate. It is important for each of us to preserve the calm of the Lodge for the sake of others, and yet when people are working with their issues, negative feelings often need to be expressed as well as positive ones. This can be disruptive!

What is the answer? How does one find peace in the midst of other people's emotional unrest? Equally important, how do we forgive ourselves if we feel we are being the disruptive ones? Well, my first piece of advice to anyone starting in the Lodge and coming up against other people's emotional demands is neither to put the Lodge or anyone in it on a pedestal, and think it or they can be absolutely perfect, nor to believe the worst of anyone either, since the ways in which they change in this environment are remarkable. And the same applies to ourselves! My second is to remember that it is part of White Eagle's teaching that we learn *brotherhood*, not just tranquillity, and that the intention is that the Lodge should be a microcosm of the outer world in that issues still have to be faced, but at least should be *somewhat* a refuge, and generally a much safer, contained space than the outside world. (I might add, to reassure, that while I would advocate tolerance of *people* unquestioningly, there are plenty of forms of behaviour which are not permissible within the sanctuary of the Lodge, and that to preserve the quiet *as far as possible* is one that is asked of everyone!) Yet again, all things do have their purpose: to have a difficult experience *wherever* you have it carries its own creative power.

This balance of acceptance of others and positive involvement in one's own process of change is not easy to achieve but it is a challenge which, I believe, meets everyone who comes to the Lodge. In this book I not infrequently set a high ideal for each of us but I do not expect instant perfection of myself or anyone else: rather, I simply try to give a little help in the achieving of it. My father—whose mystical vision has lasted and grown throughout his long life—once told me the story of how, many years ago, he had written for spiritual help to the poet 'A. E.' (George Russell). A. E. gave him the quite severe advice that for every step that we take on the spiritual path, it is necessary to take two at the physical. Probably the way in which I am most grateful for the sort of teaching White Eagle provides is that the inner focus on the light he advocates, coupled with the opportunity to learn brotherhood in a slightly enclosed space like the Lodge as well as in the everyday world, is a perfect combination in this task.

I would also say (in the spirit of A. E.'s advice) that it is all too easy to get so caught up in 'being spiritual' that we become quite woolly-headed. To have a clear view of something is not to exchange the intellectual view for the emotional. Humanity as a whole is on a path of learning, and does not need to reject all it has learnt to follow spirit. Scientific advances need not be shunned, nor need we deny the ability of education to inform our attitudes. In our work in the Lodge, for instance, I believe we can be much helped by constant outward attention to the highest standards humanity has set itself—which on the way may well include issues like professional standards. Recognizing what others have taken from experience, we need to re-examine our attitudes, and the way we present ourselves, as often as we can. I recall a member once saying to me that what had attracted him to the Lodge first, many years ago, was how completely free of prejudice it was in the matter of divorce (a freedom which in much of secular society today is taken absolutely for granted). Other prejudices are just as easily adopted, however, though the issues have changed, and sometimes a little outward-looking intellectual awareness is useful! Without it, we might for instance go through our lives without ever owning the ways in which, through language and convention, the social balance has promoted the dominance of the male over the female. White Eagle's teaching very strongly seeks to reawaken the feminine part in all of us. So it is part of my endeavour in this book to take a fresh look at what prejudices and veiled attitudes might exist unnoticed. The mind may help, yet tolerance and clarity come from within. 'The eyes of the spirit' can never be prejudiced, for they must see only the real.

## Using the spirit perspective

Sometimes people look to White Eagle and to the Lodge for answers to the big social and political issues such as those mentioned on p. 42, and perhaps for the Lodge to take a moral lead with them. What answers does White Eagle offer? Of course, everyone will immediately spring to their own view (as do I), but what White Eagle advises is that we turn to our own spirit vision, not our earthly standards, and then we cannot help but speak from inner enlightenment, not from prejudice. One of the things that he repeats most frequently is that none of us can judge another's behaviour: even he, with his enhanced viewpoint, cannot judge. 'We dare not judge, knowing that the one whom we may be tempted to judge is merely an instrument of the divine law' (SPIRITUAL UNFOLDMENT 4, p. 18).

Aside from the Christian injunction against judging, the point is that we cannot know another's circumstances—neither his or her developmental needs nor even stage of development. Those needs may be for experiences which would normally make us shudder. Such experiences are created for the purpose of growth, and may involve some particular service, which positively requires those dark and abysmal conditions for it to happen. There may be a sacrificial element. Maybe all of us, at one time or another, need to have touched the bottom of the pond of life in order eventually to know the *full* glory of the lily which arises from that same mud.

As an example I would direct the reader to a discussion of part of St John's gospel wherein White Eagle speaks of the betrayal of Jesus by Judas Iscariot as something akin to a karmic pact. Indeed, strikingly, he describes it as 'one of the most perfect examples of true brotherhood or divine love'. Such an extreme example challenges everyday understanding! What White Eagle suggests is that Judas had karma to repay and that Jesus chose to take that karma to himself 'so that he might forgive Judas, return love for hate, and thereby break a sequence which might have gone on for ages'. As White Eagle says, 'It seems almost as if the Master selected Judas from among the disciples to betray him' (THE LIVING WORD OF ST JOHN, pp. 113–14).

I also recall (and it may be of some comfort to those who hear the voice of guilt beside them, telling them that they are doing wrong) how White Eagle conveys through another image involving a pond how there are times when it is simply the quickest line of soul development to go straight into difficult experience, and not carefully to try and avoid it.

*It is natural to want to know what is coming along, especially with the idea that if only we knew, we could avoid certain pitfalls—for it is more comfortable to make a detour round a pond than to fall in. But if dropping into the pond is going to teach you to swim, if dropping into a spiritual pond is going to bring you illumination, or give you something beautiful— well! do not take that comfortable path round the pond!*

Perhaps the subtlety of this perspective will come out all the more if we examine for a moment White Eagle's teaching about the family. He honours the family unit very deeply, both as a symbol and as a pattern for life—the way he generally construes the Christian trinity is in the vocabulary of Father, Mother and Son—and he regards the family as the social unit in which most of the learning we do in our lives takes place. He would certainly endorse the need of every child for strong, balanced parenting with both the masculine and the feminine roles represented, to the extent that in THE WAY OF THE SUN there is a beautiful passage reminding us of the influence brought at Christmas by the divine Mother, pouring forth 'the love, the joy and the sweetness of the spiritual life' (p. 88). 'Every season', he says, 'has its own spiritual significance, but of them all Christmas is the greatest, for it binds the human family together as the heavenly family is bound' (p. 89). And the family structure, headed by the intuitive wisdom of the mother as much as by the vision of the father, is his chosen pattern for the Lodge.

Yet he sees with the eyes of the spirit, and I suspect that when *we* do, the first thing that becomes apparent is that those masculine and feminine parental roles are not strictly tied to the male and female bodies. White Eagle makes it quite clear that each one of us has a masculine and a feminine aspect within, and that in some way a true balancing of the two aspects is something

---

*Both of the images involving a pond are to be found in SPIRITUAL UNFOLDMENT 4, the lily image on p. 44 and this quotation on p. 6.

each of us has to find. This may lead us into some surprising changes of attitude. Life often drops us into the pond and leaves us to swim for it! The experience and others like it succeed in giving us a full range of sympathies and a balance between the creative and the responsive, the active and the passive selves. Physical life does not represent a finished picture but a school in which each one of us is on a course of soul development. Society, by contrast, has a way of seeking to make life safe for itself. It therefore loves to concoct rules and patterns. White Eagle would, I think, say that ultimately the experience of life forces us to find our safety in inner, not outer truth, and that that is our real armour (if we need one at all).

In the terms of individual development over many lifetimes, a strong imbalance of gender type one way or another may therefore be exactly what the soul needs. That might apply to the parenting chosen, or to the sexual orientation of the individual, or both. It might even lead to a soul feeling trapped with all the feelings of a woman inside a man's body, or vice versa. Life is infinitely varied, yet all things are from the same source. It is in accord with White Eagle's teaching that anyone is entitled to their own expression of self, and to our respect.

In the Native American tradition it was common for the homosexuals of the tribe to be accorded a special role or status, the chosen name being *heyoka.** That is but one example of respect being granted. This said, I think we need to be very awake to the difference between a true spiritual perspective and a social one, and how rooted in history (and how liable to change, too) the social one can be. A *spiritual* perspective requires a constant coming back to the non-judgmental, all-comprehending centre. The moment we judge we tie ourselves to history. Convention moves

---

*The term actually means 'spirits that do everything backwards' and is not *specific* to gay people.

on and we are left standing. I could believe that when Joan Hodgson wrote her book WHY ON EARTH in 1964 (in some ways, a precursor of the present volume), there was an expectation that she would uphold certain social principles or show that the spiritual 'law' reinforced them. Actually I do not think the spiritual law can ever uphold a principle devised by society: it can only bring a renewed sense of value to everything we do, or claim the most fundamental qualities, such as love, as timeless. Thus in writing of sexual mores the best passages in my aunt's book, I think, are where she gives this sense of value: for example in describing the sexual urge as something to be experienced, mastered and used creatively, 'until, when perfect balance is achieved, the whole being becomes illumined and transformed'.*

White Eagle himself is notably quiet about matters surrounding sex, although he may have been a little more forthcoming in private interviews, when he knew his remarks were less likely to be taken out of context. Maybe he does not discuss sex very much because the whole area is veiled in judgments and he wishes to avoid adding either to them or to the fears that surround the issue. Maybe we all want him, unconsciously, to reinforce our own conditioned belief, whatever it is, and he will not.

He himself points out how dependent on time and place are the moral attitudes to which we pay lip-service: 'In certain countries national customs allow behaviour which in a Christian land would be regarded as a sin'. He reminds us, as I would like to: 'The seeds which you will sow are not those of any particular sect or religion, but the products of your own innermost spirit'.†
Interestingly, Minesta's own published memories of previous lives include an Andean one in which it was quite accepted that she was to be married to her brother To-waan.* White Eagle has always advocated that we should enjoy life, including the gifts of

*1979 edition, p. 117.    †*Angelus*, October 1943, p. 14.

the body we inhabit, but also that we should honour that body in every appropriate way. It is up to us, I think, to determine for ourselves, using earthly wisdom, what balance this implies.

There is just one thing that White Eagle says in the sexual area of debate that really stands out, which is that nothing in life is done without accompanying responsibility. In this respect his gentle understanding can give way to something surprisingly stern, though only within the framework of a warning that the subtler responsibilities are all too easily forgotten. If it would help to have an example of how this gentleness and severity go hand in hand, then let me suggest a sequence beginning with the fathering of a child. I believe White Eagle would tell us that this creates a soul memory which leads the father to know his responsibility to his offspring. The circumstances of this life and his own chosen path may not lead him to fulfil the responsibility of fatherhood at the time. He perhaps runs away from it.

The memory is still held, however. I think it would be interpreting White Eagle too closely to say categorically that that responsibility would be recreated in another life, but there seems beauty, at least, in the thought that the child's sense of the loss of its father, and the father's memory of never knowing his child, would lead the two to find one another again and in another life enjoy some or all of the lost opportunity. In my saying this, there is no passport to easy conscience. The path that begins with the denial of responsibility may be a very hard one involving great suffering and unhappiness, inflicted and self-inflicted.

Yet we actually *do not know*. Maybe every soul is different in the way it chooses to learn. White Eagle says the only 'last judgment' that takes place is when we ourselves look down on our life with great clarity and see from beyond death what remains to be achieved. That does not necessarily mean that we judge

*See THE ILLUMINED ONES, p. 39.

with bitterness and in a self-punishing way, though we might have done so in this life. Ultimately it must be that we view our life completely with love, knowing that 'all things work together for good for the soul who loves God'—another of White Eagle's favourite statements. Apparently not to work for one's own soul's good may be part of the blindness our soul chooses in this life, but ignorance does not last for ever and all *is* love.

## Sacredness

White Eagle teaches that all life is sacred—the animals and plants, the land, the sea, the sky, the rocks. Little is more sacred, however, than the relationships we make with each other. Respect arises out of the sense we have of the sacredness of the other person, even in the most mundane of relationships, such as a purely business-oriented one. Thus a sexual relationship, with its possible hope of procreation, is all the more sacred still.

Loving involvement with another person is itself creativity: it does not simply happen but arises out of the mutual desire of the persons involved to create something together, through giving and receiving. It is this deep imaginative commitment that makes it specially to be honoured. There are whole levels of creativity in a childbearing relationship that are additional, but creativity is there whatever sort of relationship it is, and regardless of whether the parties are of the opposite or the same sex. To be creative is to have one's eyes focused: creativity and love are the same. I remember as a child hearing White Eagle say—and not in this context, but illuminatingly for our lives as a whole—'Create ... create ... *create!*'.

When White Eagle says that any relationship carries with it a full measure of responsibility for both parties, again I do not think he takes a moral view, but rather says that the creativity that is put into the relationship is a lasting and powerful thing and needs to be brought right into the awareness. It needs to be felt and used all the time, not dismissed. *Awareness, feeling*: those are the sort of words White Eagle attaches himself to. *Consciously create all the time*: do not carelessly destroy, in the way that the fearful mind does. It will bring both happiness and satisfaction. Creativity that can bring a child into the world is powerful indeed, and that creation of life is inextricably involved with the setting up of karmic responsibilities. Yet they are still karmic responsibilities, not moral ones: we do not know the forces which drive other people together or apart. The sense of responsibility each parent has is instinctive; in his teaching I suppose White Eagle would simply help a parent to hear it consciously. Between the partners in the relationship he would advocate a developed sense of responsibility and caring too, but one beginning with a deep self-respect, so that while stepping out of a relationship could not lightly be done, it would also be foolish to continue in the pretence of it after it has really ceased to exist—for to be unconscious of one's duty to oneself is also to be unconscious of the harm we may be doing ourselves and each other. I remember the teacher Emmanuel, often more instantly challenging in his answers than White Eagle, responding to the question 'What shall I do with my deteriorating relationship?' with the reply: 'Let it deteriorate!'.* I don't think he meant that casually at all, but rather to be present with oneself as much in its deterioration as in its success. To walk out of relationship unscathed and truly self-aware is a tightrope path. There is sacredness in relationship, but sacredness in the way out of it, too.

The quality implied is one to which White Eagle would give the name 'acceptance'. I think that conventional usage has made this a passive quality; I hope that here it may be seen to be an

*EMMANUEL'S BOOK, p. 199.

53

active embrace of experience, not a withdrawal from it.

Notably, the vows in the White Eagle marriage service are for each party to be loyal to the other 'until your karma in this life is finished'. White Eagle recognizes that there are such things as endings, but also that deep soul commitment may last for many incarnations. And to those who fear loss, I think he would like to add that in an even deeper sense, every relationship we create with another being is for eternity. We meet our friends again and again, and through our relationships, we grow towards oneness. That is why they are *all* valuable.

The following quotation is intended not so much to promote hedonism as to assist in eradicating guilt. It is very indicative of how radically White Eagle dissociates himself from human morality to insist on a spiritual perspective. This comes from chapter two of THE PATH OF THE SOUL:

*Every time the soul does not live truth from its innermost being, it is sinning. Sin is not of the body only—indeed, the bodily sins we would not call sins at all. Sin is the failure of the soul to live truly, to express truth in thought and word and deed.*

After so unequivocal a statement, let us move on, but still in the context of sacredness. The question of drug use and abuse was relevant when WHY ON EARTH was written in 1964 and is even more relevant now. My aunt then wrote of the effect consciousness-altering drugs had on the higher bodies. (The term 'higher bodies' will not be familiar to those who read this book as their first introduction, but these are the bodies taken by the soul to enable it to function at all levels of awareness; for further amplification, see below, p. 141.) Her words read as a severe warning to the potential drug-taker and must be taken seriously.

Such a warning derives from the clairvoyant's actual ability to see these higher bodies and the effect of drugs upon them.

Minesta once wrote, in an article in *Psychic News*, of what she saw happen: 'The etheric body ... is driven away from the mastership of the higher mind, which is like sending a little ship rudderless into a stormy ocean'.

Maybe, if we were a little more confident about our own innate powers, we would be less inclined to glamorize drugs either as a substitute for true personal empowerment or as a great monster with its own enormous power. Spirit always places the power of the self before anything outside self. Yet it is salutary to remember how important a part intoxicants and hallucinogens have played in the rituals of primitive cultures through time immemorial, if only to remove some of the fears surrounding them. White Eagle does not however encourage their ritual use.

His vision is of a lifestyle which is whole and healthy, not one which is *dependent* upon anything. Here he is, in SUN-MEN OF THE AMERICAS (p. 57):

*Keep your body pure and healthy; do not allow it to be overstrained; eat wisely, of pure food, and each day open yourself to the blessing of the Christ-spirit, that your body may be illumined by the Son of God. So will you meet one another with a blessing radiating from your heart; your hands will possess the power to heal, your words to comfort those in trouble; and your very aura will show forth the radiance of the Christ-spirit, so that every soul you encounter may feel better for having come into touch with you.*

These words carry implications outside the drug context, and remind us that we poison our bodies in many ways that pass unnoticed as well as the obvious ones. It seems to me far, far preferable to have attained one's vision through a healthy, natural lifestyle and with a consciousness that has unfolded slowly, than to attain it (if indeed we can), perhaps in painfully isolated glimpses, with a vision that is so impaired we cannot enjoy the achievement or repeat it at will without drug help.

The most satisfying mountain to climb is often the one that is most difficult. This however is true in several ways. We are all at different places in our development (and have no way of telling where) and for some the overcoming of drug dependency may be precisely the mountain of difficulty that is to be climbed— with its own clear rewards. Some of this book has been written in Edinburgh, Scotland, for all its beauty a city with a tradition- ally high level of drug and alcohol abuse and a high incidence of HIV infection, as much through needle-sharing as through sexual contact. It is not untypical in that. Society often polarizes itself between permissiveness and repression; I think the spirit view stands clear of the social traps in either attitude. This is also necessary in order to develop deeper insight; for instance, to understand the effects of deprivation and hopelessness as well as the opportunities for growth therein. Some of my favourite words of White Eagle's, remembered from childhood, are to the effect that all we can really do to help other beings is 'to love them ... that is, to *understand* them'.

We talk of social problems, but need to remember that it is the individual, every time, which is real to the eyes of the spirit. White Eagle often speaks of the view of earth from spirit being like thousands—no, millions—of little lamps on a dark night. This was a most powerful message for me when I was attempt- ing to come to terms with the events in Tiananmen Square in Beijing in June 1989. Having seen China in its 'spring' a few years previously I was deeply dismayed, and shared the general horror felt in the West at the shattering of ideals we held, and the loss of life. It felt, too, like the brutal outworking of an his- torical process in which many of the human beings involved seemed not so much human as inhuman. Words, however, came to me as forcefully as anything I had felt since those I heard as a child and quoted in the Introduction to this book. They were: 'millions of individual lives working out *wonderfully*'. I believe the words came from White Eagle. I thought then of those who walked in front of the tanks, all of those whose lives reached a climax—those who in any way found greatness of heart; and also those whose lives, whose ideals, whose integrity, whose self-esteem, lay shattered. I considered the power life has to heal: to bring about healing, eventually, in everyone. Somehow the phrase seemed to take the horror out of the incomprehensible and to bring hope back. It took the horror onto a scale where, although it meant conceiving of every life separately, there could be acknowledged equally the heroism and the tragic blindness of one individual, and another, and another; and also the mixture of those qualities, the presence of both in all, the intricate complexities, and the absolute precision of spirit purpose in it.

Sometimes, in extending our sympathies to those who suffer we do not entirely give credit to the transcendent vision each soul may hold in its own tragic conditions. The sixth and seventh chapters of this book take time to describe the ideal of brotherhood which the Lodge holds and how this works in practice; most notably, how we can all have real power to influence the developing consciousness of the whole planet through our spiritual work. Yet I think it is always worth remembering that those who put themselves in apparently terrible circumstances—from the heroin addict dying of disease in an affluent society to the person dying of starvation in a poor one—have put themselves there in deep consciousness of the soul effect of what they are doing, even if they are not conscious of it at the mental level.

So, the people whom we most pity may actually be highly-evolved souls, far more advanced in understanding than we are. One of the most moving things I have read was a short story by the novelist Ben Okri about the 'singing' (an inward metaphor, really) of dying people in a drought-ridden township in Africa. It was called 'A Prayer from the Living'* and extolled the integrity of those dying as against those who looked on, for the narrator found in the dying a strange though tragic joy. It gave conviction to those souls' consciousness of the light, and they seemed to stand way above us in awareness. As I remarked earlier, *everyone* deserves our respect: pity is only part of the picture.

In the foregoing paragraphs it has been my main intention to convey that White Eagle neither offers us unshakeable judgments on most issues, nor makes us decide our own moral stance, but rather seeks to raise our vision to the extent that we see everything in its sacredness. I do not know whether in every case I have written what White Eagle would have said, or whether he would have chosen to say anything at all on certain matters. Not on every occasion is the teacher there to prop us up, and by no means to give us moral certainties. May no such certainties arise from what I have written!—but rather, the knowledge that when we do see with clear vision (true clairvoyance is seeing with the eyes of the spirit) we do not do anything other than admit again and again that we don't know. Rather than this being an excuse, I would like to suggest that it has real power. To face our intellectual limits head on with an affirmative 'I don't know' can actually be very freeing, a mantra in itself; it is indeed the beginning of meditation. White Eagle says that the first step in using the intuition is not relying on the mind. Truly not to know—not to let the mind close on an idea—is the best way to open the eyes to the spirit; it is also a kind of faith, a deep one. This is probably what I have been most grateful to learn from my teachers.

*Originally printed in *Guardian Weekend*, 11th September 1993.

# CHAPTER THREE

# The kingdom of one's self

'YOU ALL keep yourselves in bondage, in chains!', White Eagle says. 'You could be as kings, ruling supreme over all negative conditions in your lives' (GOLDEN HARVEST, p. 53). The injunction reminds me of some lines I once learned, written about the poet John Donne by one of his seventeenth-century contemporaries:

> *The kingdom of one's self, this he enjoyed,*
> *And his authority so well employed*
> *That never any could before become*
> *So great a monarch in so small a room.* *

A nice image of the power of inner poise. Let us now move on from the sacredness with which we regard external things to the sacredness we bring to our own innermost place. Although White Eagle's path is one of service, it is clear that the integrity of the individual and truth to one's self are paramount in his teaching. It is time to ask more clearly what is the self and what it means to be true to it. The following passage may be a useful starting point, though some of the terms will need explaining later.

> *There are many aspects of yourself which you think are* you,

*An Elegy on Dr Donne, by Sir Lucius Cary.

*but which are not you at all. You know (although you do not always remember) that you are not your body, that your physical body is not the whole of you—just your clothing, or your 'working tool'. You say, 'I am spirit; I live after my body has been laid aside'. There are other aspects of your being, too, which survive physical death, but they are still not the real you. There are the emotions, passions, selfish desires; and these belong, not to your spirit, but to your mind, to your astral body, your desire body. They are not the real 'I'; they too are transient, and in the end will die away, even as your physical body is laid aside. But beyond and beneath all these there still remains the real 'I', the Son–Daughter of God, the light, your eternal self. You can stand aside from all the facets of the 'not self' and analyse them. But you cannot stand aside from the real self, the 'I', the Son–Daughter of God, the light. There is within you the real 'I', the Will, the divine spark, which should control the whole self, but usually souls allow themselves to be bound and ruled by the 'not I' and all the chaos around them.*

SPIRITUAL UNFOLDMENT 3, pp. 21–22

I believe that White Eagle's concept of the self, though traditional up to a point, runs beyond that of much popular psychology. *Mainly*, psychologies lack a concept of spirit, though some come close to it. My point is not to decry them but to separate clarity about our needs (which psychology very beautifully encourages) from a unifying sense of spirit, which in terms of wants and needs offers none of the limitations of definition at all. White Eagle's approach demands absolute integrity and sense of self, but a greater feeling too that the boundaries which separate us do not ultimately exist.

Even in defining our own needs, a clear vision is required to establish what they really are. It is very easy to feel defensive of particular needs we may have, where in fact the deeper wisdom contains an altogether greater vision that is not being noticed. Sometimes we feel we need to defend our personal space. This may be very necessary; or the defence itself may be because we are listening to some voice outside the self which says we ought to do so. The true self always exists away from this axis.

Let me offer an example to show how subtle this can be. I am climbing a mountain. My reasons for doing so may be for self-esteem, for my health, to give me the chance to feel more attractive to others; it may be to satisfy another person in some way. I may have complex thoughts about it—conscience saying that I should be working, or helping a weaker member of the party lower down the hillside. That is a lot of gods I am trying to appease! Do any of them need to be appeased, or is there, somewhere beneath all these motives, a real me which simply knows what I seek, and leads me to do it? I think there is, just as there is a Zen-like answer to why I climb it in the first place (probably beyond words, but not far from Mallory's famous remark 'Because it's there'!). I think the deep me has a sense of all the little 'me's that are represented by the separate 'gods' and gives none of them just too much power because that way it remains in control. The deep me knows exactly what it wants to do, or not do. There are levels and levels of hearing, and sometimes a little practice in identifying them is a wonderful help.

What White Eagle identifies by 'the real I' is thus different from standing up for one's rights, and even discovery of our deeper motives might not be a full substitute for hearing the voice of the self. What that self has to say may be beyond words, but there may be a knowing which comes with it, progressively recognizable, which simply reassures us that what we are doing, however strange, is right. There is a spiritual vocabulary to describe the difference between (on the one hand) the wordless voice of inner poise and control and (on the other) the nearest the mind can get to that. Perhaps the term that works best for the real self is the 'I am'. *I am ... the God in me.* This all-powerful self is characterized by its serenity, and it is always there to be found, White Eagle says.

Sometimes to hear and know the true self is the most difficult thing to do, or so it seems. We are so heavily trained to hear voices *outside* ourselves—social convention, other people's projections, and so on—or to believe that our fears about existence and survival have to be met, that the one voice that is inaudible is our own. Most of us have a deep confusion around the love that we believe it is right to invite into our lives (yet how could we bring it to others if we did not allow it for ourselves?) and selfishness. A careless reading of White Eagle's teaching might even add to this confusion. Let me therefore begin by saying that there is a clear but thin line between the kind of self-consciousness that is truth, and the kind that is really self-absorption. Discovering our deepest motivation often relies as much on self-forgetfulness as self-scrutiny. Hear it carefully when (in THE PATH OF THE SOUL) White Eagle says, 'Cultivate the art of loving others and not yourself. Self-consciousness is darkness'.

I do not think he intends 'self-consciousness' to mean the deep consciousness of the divine self, but the sort of trapped self-consciousness that we feel, for instance, in an embarrassing situation. To mind *that much* about ourselves is not liberating, but rather the opposite. A process of growth leads us from narrow self-consciousness into an awareness of greater self, which simply does not know the boundaries that we ordinarily feel. The next words of White Eagle's (from the same source) are designed to take us out of ourselves in their limitations. It is true that we need to bring love to the self, but not indulgently.

*Let us consider the symbol of a lighted candle: the wick burns brightly, and little by little the wax around that flame dissolves and burns away. In a similar manner the flame of divine love by degrees consumes the lower self.... What love does in life is to transform it.*

True love of the self transforms the self.

The next chapter is deliberately about techniques such as meditation which are designed to help in distinguishing between identification with self and self-absorption. For the moment, I should like to simply to suggest that without acquiring such a technique, there are ways closer to normal everyday life that can help us find our deeper being. To do this is not selfish, and is the most loving way of all by which to help the whole of life.

Surprisingly, a good first step is to note precisely what makes us happy. Not what we think *would* make us happy—the new relationship or the dream trip to Florida—but what actually *does* make us happy. One side-effect may be to increase our happiness because we notice it more! Real happiness is very close to truth itself, White Eagle tells us. So, by training ourselves to see our happiness it becomes a little easier to choose for ourselves in the present moment exactly what it would be most loving to give to ourselves.

That will not automatically be selfish. The point is always to keep in touch with our real sense of choice, not to dull ourselves by indulgence or habit. By example, one morning recently I chose on the spur of the moment to go for a run. Doing it was something I had wanted to achieve for a while, and when I came back, it turned out not only to have benefited my own concentration and creativity extraordinarily well, but also to have fitted exactly and unexpectedly with everyone else's schedules. What I feared might carry a tinge of selfishness, proved to be just the right thing to do: I had heard the need and acted upon it.

The process in this tiny incident was almost free of actual

thought, virtually spontaneous. Yet at another moment the deeper voice of self might say: 'I know that in this moment I have the opportunity to do something which, though not obviously for happiness, and perhaps surprising to others, will initiate a transformation of myself and people about me and bring long-term happiness'. Life is a constant succession of these moments, and one of the ways in which we best learn to hear our true selves is to ask the question of what we want continually and habitually. If it brings up a string of desires, then to question further and ask what is behind those desires, will lead us back to, not away from, God.

## Deep self-motivation

I think deep self-motivation, that is, moving confidently when we hear our voice at the most profound level, is very powerful and much to be trusted; it is not selfish in the conventional sense. Often, surprisingly, it is there in what we do spontaneously rather than in careful consideration. It will not stop us doing acts of great kindness for other people, for those may be exactly what we want to do; but awareness of it will keep us always in touch with the God within, whereas conventional self-forgetfulness will take us away from it. White Eagle often speaks of cultivating self-forgetfulness, but I think he means it in the sense of forgetting the insistent desire nature at its shallow level, and certainly not a forgetfulness of the self which is really the God in us. That would be self-abandonment, a very different thing.

Nothing, indeed, is more productive of ill-health than never to listen to ourselves and our deep needs. Not to listen allows us to be driven by things outside of ourselves, such as work pressures or the pressures of human emotions. Often the function of illness seems to be to provide an opportunity to get back in touch with those deep needs. They may be perfectly simple needs, and hearing them may indeed reinforce us in a sense that what we are doing is right. Always to be in touch with them means that everything we do has the power of conviction behind it.

I recently had a particularly clear example of the difference between loss of self and honouring of self. Spending time with friends, I found that there were certain days when I allowed the awe we so often have for other people—how much more self-controlled, how much better-looking, how much our intellectual betters!—to intrude heavily upon my own sense of self, to the extent that I judged myself through what I believed would have been their eyes, and held their wisdom above my own. It led to an emotional frailty in which I not only felt sorry for myself but believed that the others were judging me adversely and behaving accordingly. What was magical to me was how, when I saw this process clearly and reminded myself of my own integrity and of the divine self expressing itself through me, not only did my own sense of self improve but the others actually seemed to be regarding me differently. I gave myself, by conscious decision, the love I divinely deserved, and it came to me from outside as well as inside.

Self-examination thus need not be a critical thing, but can be a constructive one. Just as it pays to understand our needs, it certainly does not pay to blame ourselves for not hearing them, however. It may be comforting to remember that in order to heal a situation when we seem to have lost touch with our self, the present is the only thing that matters. It only requires hearing our needs now, not going back into the past and thinking we went wrong at some point. Illness, if the cause is as I suggest, is in fact up to a point a friend; avoiding it is even better!

Being in touch with one's self is the same as living absolutely in the present at any moment. It is not 'What will happen if I do this?' or 'Where did I make a mistake?' but 'Who am I and what do I feel, *now*?'. Sometimes most valuable things can be done—in terms both of outward achievement and inner growth of understanding—merely by stopping to attend to what we feel.

White Eagle renders the whole thing uncomplex by treating it as a matter mainly of efficiency. Although this passage seems to be about something different, it is also a practical demonstration of what listening to the self both entails and enables us to achieve.

*Often you are upset and disturbed because so many things are awaiting your attention, and you work too hard in your mind. You do a piece of work a hundred times mentally when you need actually do it only once. You say to yourself again and again: 'I must do so and so,' but 'so and so' does not get done. Train yourself, then, to meet the work of the moment when it comes, and quietly do it.*

SPIRITUAL UNFOLDMENT 1, p. 19

White Eagle's message is about how we respond to things: he speaks in the same section of 'the quiet acceptance of what comes along, and doing it at the moment and finishing with it'. What a wonderful ideal! Yet it is not entirely outside our grasp. Some of the things that we come upon in our daily experience do not belong to us to deal with, but are other people's. To be alive to what really does need doing, and to train ourselves to identify what is actually our lack of faith in other people, removes an enormous amount of stress from our lives. Often we build huge unnecessary tasks for ourselves by trying to control events where a simple trust in the outworking of the divine plan (to use White Eagle's phrase) would—besides being less painful—be much more efficient. There is no need to control external events; the secret is to master ourselves within.

Learning to know oneself is a long process. It almost certainly involves setting aside certain times to focus upon it, or better still taking the moment spontaneously when it seems right to do so. The encouraging thing, though, is that everything you do consciously is right as far as this process is concerned, for then you are in touch with what is driving you. Sometimes that may lead to an adjustment of what you are doing! *But you cannot actually go wrong.* The only time you are not helping yourself grow in understanding is when you allow yourself to be dragged along by others or by fears that are never looked at. Yet even then there is a wonderful self-correcting mechanism that takes over. You may get tired, and eventually ill, and thus coming to terms with ill-health provides you with the opportunity to re-contact yourself. So the plan of evolution is always forward; it is actually very difficult to go back on it!

White Eagle often points out that tiredness is an unnecessary concept! He speaks—and it may seem to be a challenge—of health as something we have to find for ourselves if we are to continue to unfold spiritually. The other part of the quotation at the beginning of this chapter gives the concept of being not just in touch with ourselves, but ruler within our own province or world. The word he most often uses here is 'mastery': mastery of the everyday self by the deeper self. This should not, incidentally, make us feel that our conscience is mastering us but that we are twenty times larger than we normally feel! Self-mastery is a joyous concept and not a discipline, either. Of course there *is* a discipline involved: what I have just described, the habitual and continual looking at oneself and what one's real feelings are is a discipline; but not in the sense of self-mortification! It often appears to be much easier to let things slide and not to take account of one's self or responsibility for one's actions. Yet always to remember what we are doing, why we are doing it, and—lightly—whether it feels right, leads to great fullness of life.

## Thought-control

White Eagle says,

*Always think healthily, constructively, optimistically. We do
not mean with a foolish optimism, but happily and confidently,
knowing that behind all the apparent confusion of earth life a
divine purpose is at work, evolving the spiritual qualities in
the human soul.*

SPIRITUAL UNFOLDMENT 1, p. 18

This divine purpose is most easily seen when we are in touch
and attentive, not with our true vision blurred by the habits of
conventional response. White Eagle's words lead us on from this
to the idea of thought as creative, an idea best explored separately. Here, our focus is the control of the thoughts.

We have already talked about properly hearing ourselves and
knowing our feelings, so White Eagle is not exactly talking about
the suppression or repression of them. Rather, I think, he is talking about becoming familiar with the self that is never dominated by the thoughts or the feelings; and in this lies the basic
clue to what self-mastery is about. The more we remember that
spirit is the reality, the more spirit is our inner controller. What
is problematic about repressing our thoughts when they are
closely tied to our feelings is that it represents the dominance of
the mind's designs over the body's needs. Such control cannot
go on for ever. If we dwell in the heart, wherein lies the truest
sense of being, we are alive through all the layers of self without
any layer concealing from us who we truly are.

Despite this, one aspect of White Eagle's teaching which people often find puzzling is the way he advocates holding a positive
attitude all the time. He sometimes says that we shouldn't allow
ourselves to get depressed, and if (for instance) reading a newspaper distresses us, then why read the newspaper? Today we

know that depression is caused by all sorts of things including defects in the body chemistry, and cannot necessarily be chosen or shunned at will. Rightly, we might say that for any of us to feel bad about being depressed is only going to make the depression worse. So what does White Eagle mean?

Other people may give a different answer, but I would suggest that it lies not in suppressing our emotions or giving in to them either, but simply in embracing them. This can only be done through reconnecting with our true self. The teacher Emmanuel puts the process of facing things very clearly, answering just the sort of question as the one we are asking.

*Close your eyes and welcome the heaviness. It will
lighten. In so doing, you bring your self-love into an area
that believes it will never be seen, never be heard, never
be allowed.
So walk with your heaviness, saying 'yes'.
Yes to the sadness.
Yes to the whispered longing.
Yes to the fear.
YES.* *

The two teachers would, I'm sure, agree that if there is anguish to be faced, it is best to try and move consciously away first from the fear that prevents us looking at our pain. Then we can contact the part of ourselves—the deeper part—which is loving and trusting, and use that to help us look directly at what is causing us distress. Then in turn we can deal with it in the most loving way. This is the reward of the true contact with self.

Even with clinical depression, the ability to accept it for what it is, to allow it to be a place which the soul visits for growth, may be the first insight into recovery. Then one may recognize that there is a greater reality to the self than the one that our

*EMMANUEL'S BOOK II, pp. 156–57.

69

depressed self believed. Constant reiteration of this may be necessary before recovery takes place, and many other factors may be involved, but this approach does have the advantage of not prolonging staying in the condition longer than the causes of it demand. White Eagle advocates dealing as far as we can with whatever causes the problem *now* (that is, when it presents itself, or precisely when it feels right to do so), whether this is in therapy or in daily life. Deal with it once if you can, not again and again, he would say. The memory may recur, and need dealing with each time, but it is the feelings of the present moment that we deal with each time, and this is what keeps us in touch with ourselves and gradually helps us heal.

It is worth remembering that depression arises from *not* looking at things. When they *are* looked at, accepting them and creating a plan of action to deal with the issues examined helps the depression to lift. When White Eagle advises us to be positive, I think the last thing he is saying is that we should brush our problems aside and keep a stiff upper lip. Rather, he says, through accepting that they are real (and discriminating in the process between those that are real and those that are not), we may lift ourselves into the sunlight so that we get a better look at them.

*We make it a rule, when giving advice and help, always to be constructive, to see nothing but good; and we do this even though we may be called foolishly optimistic. We know that by seeing only good, by creating good by positive thought, we can help to bring about that which is desirable and good.*

SPIRITUAL UNFOLDMENT 1, p. 134

In other words, a 'foolishly optimistic' outlook *can* be more than it seems. It is not just he that can attain this standpoint, however. From his perspective, his world and ours are not separate; we are not of a different substance from him; we can achieve exactly his consciousness. It is only we that see the separation between the two worlds. If we could only realize that!

If we really open ourselves up to what our soul most needs in the moment, it may mean taking a surprising and courageous course of action. Nonetheless to hear whatever comes from within and react appropriately is by far the best way forward. Insight is real. You may remember that I spoke about Minesta's acting on deep instruction from spirit in just the same way as I now talk of responding to our needs. To hear oneself can be genuinely as surprising as Minesta's spirit instruction was. If so, we need to be really sure who we are hearing, and in Minesta's case I think her own deep intuition and White Eagle's came together.

We are beginning, I think, to understand what is meant by the phrase 'to see with the eyes of the spirit'. To do so almost always requires a change of perspective and thus of the thought-pattern. Sometimes that will seem immensely difficult, but always when we actually do it, it feels easy. The true self or spirit goes through a vast number of experiences and is wrapped round by a complex and shifting bag of emotions. To see with the eyes of the spirit means not allowing ourselves to feel identified by who we are in the shallow sense: name, traits of character, race, age, or anything of this sort. Our identity is not our emotional state (such as depression) either. Seeing with eyes of the spirit acknowledges that we go *of our own choice* into a vast array of life-experience (including illness) for growth—and even for a greater, cosmic purpose. That purpose is to take the light that we ourselves are, into precisely the places where no light seems to exist: states like depression or the seemingly darkest and ugliest places of the physical world. When we retain a profound sense of who we are, and make that self sovereign, rather than the everyday being, we see with true spiritual clarity.

# CHAPTER FOUR

# Self-healing and healing

IT MAY BE that the suggestions in the preceding chapter seem like hard work, because they put the onus in reclaiming our personal power upon ourselves. There is, fortunately, another side to the coin, because although healing does come from within, it also comes from a universal source, and others can help in this. This is where spiritual healing comes in.

Many people come to the White Eagle Lodge for the first time to attend a healing service, though they may equally come to find a place of silence and safety and there learn a technique of meditation that will enable them to feel and use their contact with the source of life. Meditation and healing are quite closely allied, and this chapter is quite a practical one, giving some of the Lodge teaching about meditation, and leading on into the subject of healing (at which point I shall honour my promise to show that help can also come from outside!).

One of the things I personally enjoy in the Lodge is working with people in the early stages of meditation training. Partly, the enjoyment comes from confidence that the training White Eagle gives in the realization of the true self is second to none. I also find that he makes it a very natural activity, not a complex one, and this makes me happy.

When beginners come to a meditation, one of the things I therefore want to stress is that it doesn't have to be regarded as something massively different from everyday life. I believe that we do a lot of quiet meditating, daily—just by listening to sounds in nature, enjoying sunshine (or rain), catching our breath and being ourselves in an uncomplicated but attentive way. One thing all these have in common is that each of them is an appreciation of the *present*.

All that meditation does is to embrace this natural quality we have and enhance its effect. This demands only one thing, which is to become focused, away from interruption. This may seem obvious, but freedom from interruption is not only for our own sake. If someone tries to talk to us while we are meditating it is as embarrassing for them as for us. I remember with some amusement the expostulations of the local community, recorded in a British Sunday newspaper, about their encounters with groups of members of one of our sister organizations meditating in their path upon the local beach! A good reason for choosing the right time and place is in order to avoid other people feeling excluded, as well as not to run the risk of casual disturbance.

The actual experience in meditation is a heightening of something we do already, not a whole new thing. This world *is* beautiful, and does not always need surpassing! Sometimes just to gaze at a flower or a candle, and no more than that, is the most rewarding thing we can do; or to walk steadily, consciously, in the natural world, unswayed by other preoccupations, just clear about what we are doing, and doing it well. The athlete and the artist, in their concentration, are close to meditation too.

Just as the athlete or artist cannot afford to be distracted, though, it is useful for us to find a way to minimize our disturbances. We may need to hear what could distract us—traffic noise outside, for instance—and then acknowledge that our inner world is actually greater than the one defined by that noise. There is much more to our consciousness than a few internal combustion engines doing their worst! Similarly, we are bigger than our problems. We do need to let these go before we start, and this may mean for a moment knowing them; even seemingly giving in, mentally. By acknowledging our troubles in a controlled way we often succeed in cutting them down to size, and once we have stopped fighting them we often find it much easier to put them on one side. So we need just to remind ourselves that we cannot do anything to resolve this or that problem right now, and lay it down. Whatever is necessary to forget the problem has to be done, if only for an instant. For in that instant—the space between a sigh and a breathing in again—the magic can happen and the heart opens to something greater. At the moment of release, the mind (which conceives of troubles, holds on to troubles, and then wraps them in more fears) is forgotten.

After this brief preparation, we can go on. White Eagle says it helps to picture a lighted flame within one's heart, or to see a sun shining inside us. The same effect can be achieved by remembering something beautiful, like a familiar scene in the countryside. We can rest with that beauty and allow ourselves to feel the warmth inside us associated with it. It is a real feeling and it can be quite recreative.

The memory of the old conditions—be it loneliness, pain, illness, anger or sorrow—will tend to return, and it may even happen very soon. But the way to make the link with the true self, the higher self as White Eagle would call it, has been found, and it now requires only memory and practice to get back to it. The first stage in meditation has been reached.

## Our true nature

What we are touching when we allow this moment of warmth, this opening of the heart, is almost beyond definition. Once we have started practising, it goes on getting clearer, however. We may seek names for it—Brahma, God-consciousness, simple *being*—but it is what is there when the mind gets out of the way, no more and no less. We are very used to having something about us that we can define: sensory experience, mental concepts, depression. They serve as preoccupations: we rather rely on them. To be without the mind's control—what happens then? Is there a void, a blankness? No, although for a very brief moment it may seem so. In fact, in the early stages, we are very unlikely to enter this state fully anyway. It can take a lot of practice! Nonetheless, a feeling that it really is all emptiness may grip us for a moment or two. Anticipating this, White Eagle says:

*If you will train yourself in contemplation, you will find that beneath the soul [here White Eagle means the level of the receptive consciousness] there is a place of stillness, of blankness, of nothingness if you like. Yet when you are confronted with the seeming nothingness which lies beneath the conscious self, you will gradually become aware of an all-ness, a sense of affinity with universal life and at-one-ment with God. In this condition there can be no separation, no darkness, no fear: nothing exists but love and an exquisite joy which permeates your whole being.*

GOLDEN HARVEST, p. 31

White Eagle constantly seeks to help us realize our true nature. We are not, he says, only our personalities, our bodies, or our minds, but something much greater. There is a magic to this realization, for it genuinely can transform conditions of sorrow into understanding and even joy, and conditions producing illness into conditions producing health.

*The sorrows, the responsibilities, the anxieties which you think are yours, do not belong to you at all. You are that shining self, that light, that essence of being that you find in the hours of meditation.*

SPIRITUAL UNFOLDMENT 3, p. 23

Our power to take charge of our lives is huge and largely unrealized. We mainly live our lives in a shallow, time-trapped and fear-based consciousness when we could be opening ourselves to our true power and strength, and indeed beauty. For the self that we touch at the deeper level just described, although it is *our* self, does not have the same barriers that separate it from other people that the personality or lower self does. At the deepest level, the consciousness of true self is the consciousness of universality. Through knowing ourselves we know all things.

## To see ourselves for ourselves

Many of us spend our lives believing we are best defined by what other people think of us. What I have outlined here is to help us see ourselves for ourselves. Truly, we can only know ourselves by forgetting what others think and even getting away from the concept of personality altogether. Our true self is not a character to be judged from the face we see when we look in the mirror, but a self without limits and with infinite potentialities. There is no edge to it, nothing we can see from the outside, and yet our true self is by nature beautiful.

This is a mystical way of putting it, of course, but what is special about White Eagle's teaching is that he does constantly offer us a simple way of developing the consciousness so that it may grasp concepts the mind cannot grasp. First, he says, a developed inner consciousness can be found through listening, and watching. Listening to the sounds of nature or watching the expression of it can open the heart both to an inner world and, simply, to beauty. Beauty is a key because, like love, it quite spontaneously opens the heart. Beauty can be found in a great many guises—and as the heart opens, still more beauty can be found, sometimes unexpectedly. Nothing is more effective in touching the heart than the beauty of the natural world. Another symbol White Eagle offers for our contemplation beside the lighted flame in the heart is the symbol of the rose. The power of this image is in its beauty, and the serenity it brings too is a reminder of the absolutely natural way in which both the flower, and the heart, can open. As he says, 'Flowers do not force their way with great strife. Flowers open to perfection slowly in the sun' (THE QUIET MIND, p. 58).

Secondly, the ways already suggested—even the quiet contemplation of beauty—can be developed into a rather more prolonged attempt to focus in upon the true self. Here, the bridge to deeper consciousness is most easily found through the breath. This bodily function keeps going without any instruction or stimulus from our minds. In fact, the moment our minds do operate upon it we tend to rush it, gulp our breath, or in one way or another destroy or force the rhythm of breathing. White Eagle takes us, gently, through this moment, by offering us images like that of a boat on an almost still lake. As we watch any ripples subside, the breath almost inevitably follows suit. He says, 'As the still water reflects the sky, so the calm soul reflects the image of Christ' (in Grace Cooke's MEDITATION, p. 99).

Having found a place to sit quietly, without interruption, you will know that your mind is starting to be quiet when you become conscious of your natural breathing rhythm returning—and to be *consciously* aware of it is the key. Your consciousness is like the boat on the water: floating upon the unruffled surface, which is like the gentle support the breath offers you.

Simply to stay with this is a wonderful meditation in itself. Every time the thoughts wander, you can just return to aware-ness of your breath, or visually to the image of the water, if you prefer. It is a perfect training, but it is also something enormously worth doing in its own right.

## Visualization

The images described in the last few pages—first the image of the rose, and then that of the boat on the still water—form a meditation technique in themselves, that of visualization. Visu-alization is useful because it is a way of occupying the mind while turning it towards beauty, and through beauty going from men-tal consciousness to an opening of the heart. The emptying of the mind, which some disciplines suggest, White Eagle says is very difficult for the westerner to achieve.

In the present book, I am trying to offer a way of beginning meditation only, and the subject of visualization is well covered in other books from the White Eagle Publishing Trust, most im-portantly my grandmother's book THE JEWEL IN THE LOTUS, al-though her earlier MEDITATION may be a preferred place to begin. I would, however, like to offer the following passage from one of White Eagle's books because I think it most usefully shows the very simple way in which very profound concepts are brought to our senses through his teaching—and also because it intro-duces more of the classic images we may choose for visualiza-tion. It may serve as a meditation in itself, if you want to use it in that way.

*You will often hear of the symbol of the water lily being used in spiritual unfoldment. The lily shown on the surface of the water is an ancient symbol of the unfolding spiritual gifts. If you would cultivate gifts of the spirit, first close your eyes and ears to all that is physical, then create a vision, or a mental picture, of a harmonious, beautiful garden. Walk through your garden to the innermost sanctuary, passing through the wide-open gate; and within that inner garden, see the silent pool, pure and still and so clear ... still water of the spirit is clear as crystal. You may look into that water, and see the true reflection of yourself, for the waters of the spirit never lie. On the surface of the water you will see the lily, pure white, with a centre of gold—white and gold, symbolical of purity and divine intelligence. Rest quietly in contemplation of this perfect flower.*

THE GENTLE BROTHER, pp. 38–39

Such a visualization can be developed further, as you prefer.

## Meditation on the Star

White Eagle says that our meditations, because they put us back in touch with our own stillness and true self, are the beginning of healing. One of the reasons why healing services are offered within the White Eagle Lodge is to enable people to find the source of healing within themselves. Obviously it is easier to take medication, assuming that there is some well-proven drug available; but healing in the way I describe here (even in conjunction with medicines) puts the power back with the patient.

To those who suffer disease or intense pain, this may sound like something quite difficult to achieve. Sometimes to face difficulty again, and again and again, is the only way to develop a contact with the source which is so real that it transforms us. Even the smallest effort in this direction is beneficial in countering pain, and at its deepest level meditation may actually identify and help to remove the root cause of the illness. To those who claimed a pill as a short cut White Eagle, I think, would gently shake his head and perhaps smile, and say that there are no short cuts to healing at all. To believe that healing is possible in a deep or lasting sense without a development in self-awareness: that is the unreality! However, this change may happen unsought and unnoticed. One might possibly argue that some cases of miraculous healing happen so spontaneously that it is difficult to claim a change in awareness, and yet the woman to whom Jesus spoke the words *Thy faith hath made thee whole* was miraculously healed because she believed that even to touch the hem of his garment was enough.*

The ways in which this self-awareness may come are many and different, and it does not have to be describable in the language of any one person's teaching. However it is described, though, self-awareness is the start of healing and not just a nice luxury for those who have the time to seek it.

White Eagle provides further help with our meditation, and so with our inner healing, by reminding us of another symbol, namely the six-pointed Star. It is the symbol which the Lodge was given, via its predecessor the Polaire Brotherhood (see Appendix, p. 147), by those 'illumined ones' for whom White Eagle says he is the spokesman. Sometimes called the Star of Creation, it is like the Jewish Star of David but it lacks the interlacing lines. It is composed of two equilateral triangles, one pointing upward and one downward. The upward-pointing triangle symbolizes human aspiration and growth, whereas the downward one symbolizes the love or grace of God bestowed on us as we aspire. Alternatively they can be seen as our human self and our higher or celestial self. The two are totally integrated when one sees the Christ-man or Christ-woman—that is, the person with God fully realized within him or her—like the mark at the end of the furrow we walk. The intersecting lines are never shown in White Eagle's use of the symbol, so that it stands for wholeness. One may also see in the Star the beauty of the snowflake, or the magic of the Star of Bethlehem. It is a Christ symbol, but does

*See Matthew 9 : 22.

not rely on Christian doctrine for its meaning: rather, it touches on the very mystery that lies behind religion. Although it may seem strange to give a geometrical figure such significance, I hope these brief ideas have already given it some life.

So if we picture ourselves within the Star, or stand with arms outstretched and imagine ourselves creating part of the form of the Star with our bodies, we are doing something very powerful with our creative thought. We can then set our focus on becoming perfected in health, in outlook, in loving compassion, and develop this practice as we like. I particularly recommend the 'Tree of Light' breathing routine in my mother's book A WAY TO HAPPINESS (chapter seven). Perfection is not pie-in-the-sky, but something intrinsic to the whole cycle of human evolution, for White Eagle says that the road of human development leads back to happiness, not away from it. As we discover our true selves, we become happier.

Interestingly, the Star is not particularly easy to visualize. Speaking for myself, when I try to see all six points at once, then as fast as I successfully see each one in turn I tend to lose sight of all the other five. I think that this is part of what White Eagle is trying to show us, for I doubt if the mind can ever focus on all six points simultaneously (just as it can never quite perceive infinity). However, the heart can. When we try to see the Star with the heart-imagination, the mind softens its attempt to see and retain each part of the symbol. Then the Star can be potently clear and radiant, with each point in place. Try it! It is a very useful exercise in heart-concentration in itself.

This is a natural way to continue from the simple form of meditation which relies just on an awareness of our quiet breathing. Beginning with that steady concentration we can picture the Star (perhaps, it shines over the water of the first image we looked at?) and just stay with it, identifying with it, allowing it to flood us with light. The more practised we are, the longer we can stay with it. We can feel it within us, or we can feel that we actually become the Star. We can imagine it three-dimensionally, and use its geometry to see all the components of our being developed and held in balance. This becomes a way of enhancing the deep self-honouring I described on p. 65.

Eventually, we will want to return to everyday consciousness, and then it is best to use the breath again, only this time to be really aware of what the *body* is doing as we breathe, and increasingly to feel how our bodies are in contact with the chair we sit on, the floor, and the room, and so on, until we are right back among our outward perceptions.

## Continuing the healing process

Healing is a process of change, from one condition or awareness to another. It is important to stress that the *starting point* of healing is the allowing of change in the self, and that contacting the self is the best way to allow change. One can use the technique so far outlined, especially the way in which we let our troubles go and visualize ourselves within a Star, as a way of affirming the new mode of life we wish to inherit, be it health, a way forward out of difficulty, or a new awareness. It helps to be very conscious of letting the old patterns die when we breathe out, and of inviting the fresh possibilities when we breathe in. The symbolic power of the new breath can be remarkably helpful. And sometimes it is quite revealing to us to recognize how difficult it is to face changes, even for the better. Yet there is really no need to carry the old careworn self, with its history of pain and tribulations, into the next moment at all. We can actually be creators of a whole new being for ourselves with every moment that passes. The feeling of deep safety, coming from within, that the Star brings can also be a way of finding the courage to change, or to leave resentment and anguish behind.

The techniques I have described are not intended, in the case of someone who is sick, to replace medical treatment, and may indeed be something begun long after medication or surgery has been prescribed. The same is true for anyone asking for healing treatment through the White Eagle Lodge. It can be done either remotely—'Absent Healing'—or by physical attendance—'Contact Healing' (see below, pp. 158–60), but alongside it a sensible use of medical help is always advised. Alternatively, the chosen way forward, alongside the healing, may also be through some other form of complementary therapy, or through psychotherapy or counselling. Astrological counselling may prove to be useful. So may some physical practice which opens the awareness to what is out of line in the self and causing pain, a way such as yoga. Yoga means union, and as practised fully it denotes a striving for union with universal- or God-consciousness while focusing on the body itself through *asanas* (postures). The body is almost a map of the life in its aches and pains, and often to work on postures is to bring relief at a much subtler level than the surface one.

At some White Eagle Lodges and groups, Bach Flower Remedies are also prescribed as an adjunct to healing, perhaps along with counselling, though any elaboration of the treatment is kept to a minimum. Healing by the spirit, that is by the rediscovery of the true life-force—is a way of healing best kept very focused.

On its own the White Eagle healing uses nothing but the absolute power of the God, or Oneness, within us. It draws upon a power that is far stronger than any illness or condition, and is universal and immediate in its application. In the words of the White Eagle Contact Healing Service:

*The life of God is within you ... and as you learn to say, deeply and strongly, from the Christ within your heart, 'I am the Resurrection and the Life' that life-force rises within you. Every particle, every cell of the body is subject to the divine power and glory.*

*Hold fast to the certainty that Christ within you is king, and can overcome all weakness, all sickness, all inharmony....* True spiritual healing can work with any other therapeutic programme, but it is in itself magical and can be quite immediate in its physical effect.

White Eagle teaches that the power of thought is the most significant thing in healing. There are many ways in which this is true, and the next chapter explores some of them. However, the level of thought which the healing touches is not 'positive thought' as generally understood. A positive attitude is certainly helpful, but the attunement that we as seekers after healing can make with our own inner healer, or with the universal healing principle, requires a stillness of mind, not an effort of will.

## Giving healing

Returning in our thought to the symbol of the Star, we may recall its power in signifying the perfect self, man–woman made perfect. Meditation can be taken further, so that our consciousness is wholly in the universal light and we take communion with the source of life. White Eagle teaches that it is not a complex matter to do this, rather something we can do easily, though the more easily with practice. Such a communion, simply led, is a feature of all the main White Eagle services. 'The power of the spirit is within you. It is creative and knows no limitation.... Never allow yourself to feel the limitations of physical matter.... As you think, so you *are*' (HEAL THYSELF, pp. 55–56).

In using the Star as a symbol of perfection, we can as easily see another person as we can see ourselves, touched by the rays of light from that symbol. We may see them standing—whole and healed—within it. The process by which we seek healing for another person is the same as it is for bringing healing to ourselves. In the language of the healing work of the Lodge, we see them 'whole and perfect in the light'. The light of the Star is often at its most effective in healing problems within relationships, and can also be used to bring healing to areas of conflict in the world, or to the planet itself to bring about ecological balance, or to help bring harmony between races or peoples.

While it is not too difficult to see how the healing works in ourselves—for the change in our attitude itself could promote the healing—how can it work for other people and conditions? For an explanation from a totally different source I should like to turn to the words of the Indian Vedanta teacher Vivekananda, whose word *prana* describes the life-force.

*Every part of the body can be filled with prana, the vital force, and when you are able to do that, you can control the whole body. All the sickness and misery felt in the body will be perfectly controlled. Not only so, but you will be able to control [the healing of] another's body.... There have been cases where this process has been carried on at a distance. But in reality there is no distance which admits gaps. Is there a gap between you and the sun? There is continuous mass of matter, the sun being one part, and you another.... Prana can be transmitted to a very great distance.... The pure-souled man who has controlled his prana has the power to bring it into a certain state of vibration which can be conveyed to others, arousing in them a similar state of vibration.*

RAJA YOGA, pp. 42–44

White Eagle's teaching is that we cannot fully achieve our own healing without focusing also upon the healing of the world.

The world about us interacts with our inner selves through our worries, our ideas, our emotions. If we heal our environment, we are healing our lives too; if we heal conditions like violence in society we are working upon our own inner selves, and vice versa. Most importantly, though, we do contain the world inside us. This concept is one which the ancient mystical tradition calls the microcosm and the macrocosm. Our true consciousness is both microcosm (our own little world) and macrocosm (the vast world). A moment's thought establishes this—we only have to shut our eyes and think about the whole world to embrace it, perhaps most creatively, in our thoughts. Our consciousness therefore is not only individual but also universal, and so we can heal the world *through* our selves, through our inner consciousness. It *is* within us: it doesn't just seem to be. For all this, it may be an easier concept actually to visualize the world as external, and to shine the light outwards or downwards upon it.

To live in the consciousness of a healed self and a healed world, a perfect self and a perfect world, is something ultimately to be done not only in times of crisis and despair, but every minute of every day. Because this sounds like impossibility—though perhaps it is not, really—White Eagle has suggested that we make a point of holding this focus of the earth and all its people within the perfect light of the Star. He suggests a programme of doing this every three hours, at what he calls the magical hours, namely 3.00, 6.00, 9.00 and 12.00. To practise opening the heart to a vision of a healed world and a healed self as frequently as this is to establish a wonderful discipline for the consciousness which can and does change lives. It is something not to be seen as a duty but something in which we can participate at will. After all, it works through the inner will and only if this is present will it work. The greatest power on earth comes from the alignment of the individual will with the divine will.

# CHAPTER FIVE

# The creative power of thought

TO MAKE any progress in developing self-awareness and to stand a good chance of being able to lay on one side the obstacles preventing the healing of self, it is helpful to have a way of explaining the conditions in which we find ourselves. The principal way White Eagle does this is through the idea of karma. Karma is a doctrine which much of the new age movement pays lip-service to; I should like to show that White Eagle's teaching about it is actually quite subtle, and possibly subtler than is generally supposed.

First, a reminder that because White Eagle is a teacher who wishes to free us to our own inner truth, he does stress that nothing he says carries a requirement of belief. If you read his words closely, I think you will find that he is prepared just fractionally to undermine the certainty of what he teaches, perhaps with a remark implying that we have to arrive at our own understanding on a particular issue. You will find this particularly true when I come to speak of reincarnation in chapter six. In an early teaching which I quote there more fully, he reminds us: 'It is impossible to convey in earth language the inner mysteries of life. You must work, as all pupils must, for yourselves, and frame your own conception of truth.'

There and elsewhere, he is not afraid of leaving something as a paradox if he feels it is more useful to do so. If he speaks of the coming of a new world teacher or a coming again of the Christ as teacher upon the earth, sometimes it feels as though this teacher is to be realized in our hearts, and sometimes he seems to speak of an actual being drawing close to manifestation. Maybe from spirit the distinction is less clear; at any rate, to state either categorically might leave us far less involved in our own destiny.

White Eagle's teaching about karma follows a similar pattern. Let us begin simply. Popularly in the West, the doctrine is not very far removed from St Paul's *As ye sow so shall ye also reap* (Galatians 6 : 7). In other words it is about the result of action. In the extreme use of the word it seems to be almost about punishment, and at the least it is thought to be about the inherited consequences of action, good or bad. In fact *karma*, which is a word from Hinduism much enriched by Buddhist teachings, simply means action—or to be more precise, action which has the will behind it. The whole sense of it being about the result of action has been added to it since.

This appropriation of the word is not wholly without roots in Hinduism itself. Hinduism has another word, dharma, which means duty to one's path.* That of course can be taken in many different ways (the caste system is an extreme one among them), but there is overall an idea that bad karma, wrong action, arises out of failure to be true to dharma, in this context meaning one's self. Maybe it is apparent from this how, colloquially, we might talk about 'bad karma' to imply what consequences are generated by the failure to be true to one's self.

---

*In Buddhism it rather means 'teaching'—both 'the teaching' and 'inward teaching'.

Although he often assumes the popular western understanding of the word, in keeping a causal aspect to it, White Eagle nonetheless takes it beyond 'action'. He teaches that the basis of everything lies in thought. Action begins with thought, and so does our destiny and our wellbeing. Even our bodies are controlled by how we think about them.

I have tried to make it clear that this is how healing works; attuning the thought to the divine consciousness enables the divine consciousness to work through the body. Yet one of the obstacles to healing is the belief that we cannot get better. This can be acquired accidentally from the way we understand science (for instance, from our doctors), from our childhood history (from our parents or schooling), from more recent experience, or perhaps from believing too literally in a determinist view of life. The idea of karma has in some places (including India) taken on this colour. In other words—so goes the narrow application—the difficulties of this life are something we created for ourselves through action in past lives, and until this accumulated karma is worked through there is very little we can do. 'Oh, it's my karma' is the typical cliché.

Yet White Eagle does not teach this, and what he says instead, and with great insistence, is that we create the conditions of our lives not so much by our actions as by our thoughts. (There are parallels in Jesus' teaching, too, in the sermon on the mount and elsewhere.) While an action, when done, apparently cannot be reversed—hence the apprehension that karma is absolutely binding—thoughts are endlessly open to change and renewal. In fact the action has gone: whether thought of as 'good' or 'bad', it is finished with, not us any longer; but thought, as consciousness, remains real, creative. It is *us* far more than action is.

Another way to discover the flexibility of what we call karma is to remember what White Eagle teaches about there being no time in spirit, and no distance either. To believe that karma is punitive, which is so often done, relies on a sense of time being linear: we reap the consequences of things past. White Eagle teaches that time is in fact an illusion which is unique to the physical plane. Interestingly, modern science has begun to deny the linear notion of time too. Time is a useful tool with which to look at the running of our lives, including the consequence of thought, but in no sense is it actually real. It is difficult to avoid using language which presupposes linear time, but I suggest that the more we can ignore time the better we shall understand White Eagle's teaching on karma.

Even using that language, White Eagle speaks of some karma as being instantaneous. This is something we recognize from personal experience. If we are in control of our being, happiness shines from us and all that comes to us seems to be good. He would call this karma just as much as any cramping condition in our lives inherited from the so-called past. If, rather than our lives coming after one another in sequence there is actually a 'now' in which we can think as we will, we are absolutely able and free to create, in a positive sense, all the time. So if we inject love, forgiveness, into a situation that is apparently past we actually do transmute it. But it does not mean going back into the past or into another place to do so. The time we do that is now.

Basically, White Eagle teaches that the overriding law is love, not what people have come to call karma. There is no law of punishment. He uses the word karma to describe what brings opportunity into our lives, though sometimes he prefers the word dharma for this. The two words between them describe the teaching that life itself brings us, and the opportunities we create for ourselves. Karma is always better seen as opportunity than as imprisonment, for in the former we are in touch with ourselves, and in the latter we are powerless before the force of destiny. He says that if you believe karma is inexorable you are *missing the crux of the whole matter. Do not accept suffering, limitation, hardship, difficulty, as something ordained, inescapable, for this other law [of opportunity] operates side by side with that of cause and effect.* From an unpublished teaching of 26th July 1955 Maybe karma is more akin to a memory: an inner record of the things we feel we have not done quite right, the things we feel are incomplete (I cannot avoid the vocabulary of linear time here!). Because of the soul urge to bring all to perfection, we bring precisely the events before us to enable us to work upon what feels less than perfect. But our attitude to the events (and to the soul memory) remains absolutely free. White Eagle would say that we can either imprison ourselves by our thoughts or liberate ourselves from the prison-house of circumstance. We can give ourselves lives of pain and misery, or with knowledge we can give ourselves lives of joy.

At the same time, he says, the earth genuinely *is* a place designed for learning. Coming into incarnation is to enter into a life whose individual designer is the spirit of the individual itself. When someone has a particularly difficult experience it is extraordinarily short-sighted to say that it came to them as retribution, through 'bad karma', or even through negative thoughts of any sort. The experience provided absolutely the right opportunity for soul development. White Eagle teaches us that everything in life is creative; there is no waste or randomness in it. 'It is through what you call bad karma that you gain wisdom.' We may have a difficult life, but not so much to punish ourselves as out of a deep desire to learn, whether or not in the process we are 'paying something off'. Our karma, to use the word in the sense of the things we have created, gives us opportunities beyond all measure for spiritual growth.

91

Here is another defining passage. I cannot avoid the concept of time, and no more does White Eagle manage to express the concept of karma here without using the illusion. Read it knowing this, and with the sense that we sow thought, not action.

*My brethren, you have all helped to create your present world. You will disagree at the outset with this statement, but it is true. You have also created your own body. You will say, 'Oh no, that is impossible'. Yet the human body changes all its atoms every seven years. Every seven years you have a totally new body, created during those seven years. During every new incarnation, whether you like it or not, you inherit the conditions you have sown in your past. Even in this present incarnation you create the conditions in which you live today. You disagree again? Let us survey your home surroundings, the clothes you wear, the books you read, the recreation you enjoy. All these things are manifestations of your spirit, your own choice. You will say, 'Oh, but I did not choose my kind of work. I did not choose the companions I find uncongenial'. Make no mistake, my dear brother–sister; you have created your conditions. Once you have seen that fairly and squarely, and really accept the fact with courage and sweet surrender to the wisdom and love of God, you can set about developing the divine within you, and create on a higher level, on a higher vibration, a life which proves harmonious, beautiful and happy.*

Angelus, October 1946, pp. 206–207

## Recreating our world

White Eagle tells us furthermore that the whole point of human life is to bring love into every possible situation. It is to see beauty, to see God, in all things. This is precisely what he describes as 'seeing with the eyes of the spirit'. 'Yes, even in that which appears to be unenlightened, may we see the beauty of Thy work.' The sentence is from one of his best-known prayers.* He would perhaps remind us therefore that a difficult life may be the most deeply loving thing a soul can offer itself—the opportunity to bring its love to bear upon the darkest condition, and to move forward through a huge growth in knowledge. I hope this is comforting. Sometimes deep suffering is the only way in which a soul truly finds itself. The moment can otherwise be put off and put off, until whatever might be found within becomes something we really fear. Suffering forces us to confront our own utter depths. However much, initially, we may regard them with self-horror, we stop, look, and when we look down into the abyss we find it contains not a monster but a being of love.

The concept of life as opportunity is another reason it is inappropriate to judge another person (or ourselves) either by apparent karma or by personality. We come into incarnation with specific work to do, a task often quite unknowable at the level of human personality. White Eagle often speaks of the individualized spirit as a jewel, whose facets need to be polished one by one: the rough personality may be one uncut or unpolished facet that alone is incarnating at the present time, with a great jewel of richly acquired experience unseen behind it. When we really allow ourselves to see this jewel we see ourselves as we truly are, and we see other people as *they* truly are. True understanding of being is a recognition of beauty.

The idea of being able to create by our thoughts is one quite commonly held in new age circles. It is probably worth seeing the disadvantages of this as well as the advantages. The drawback is that once we regard everything as being of our own choosing it can become yet another rod with which to beat ourselves.

*PRAYER IN THE NEW AGE, p. 31.

Not only do our lives go wrong but it's all our fault for letting them go that way! Moreover, it becomes very easy to regard someone else's misfortune as of their own making, and harshly to back away from sympathetic understanding.

In other words, while to regard things as our own choice can be re-empowering, real imagination is required in doing this. It requires an understanding of what facet of our being we are trying to polish when we look back, perhaps initially with regret, on what we have chosen. If we are to understand it fully we need to re-enter the moment of choice itself and go right into the context of what we were trying to achieve. The same applies to how we look at another person, although I think it is necessary to admit that even the deepest sympathetic understanding can never do this fully.

I think White Eagle would tell us that some choices of life-circumstance are made before birth, some after. In the case of the former, then the intended growth purpose is inevitably difficult for human reasoning to grasp during the life. After birth we are largely blind to what went on before. In the case of choices made after birth, then it is as well to remember that the choice may still have been made at a very deep, subconscious level, much more in touch with the wisdom of the higher self than with what the everyday mind would notice. At a later date, how can the consciousness possibly recapture fully what it scarcely knew even at the time? So to make what later seems like a curious choice is not to have let ourselves down. Probably, it was the most loving way forward, however unlikely that may seem later.

Although one can never really know another's karma, any growth in understanding brought by difficult circumstances is comforting both to the person at the centre of it and to others. Sometimes the growth suffering brings is the only clue we have to why the choice was made in the first place. Not so long ago a letter came to the Lodge from someone serving a life sentence in prison, who described what had happened to him through being given the opportunity, by his life-circumstances, to reflect and change. He was then working out for himself, progressively, what his continuing life might offer.

*My actions cost a man his life, but I can now face that; it is a debt I will someday have to repay, it's the law, but at last my conscience hasn't given me such a hard time these past few years. I feel as if I have been forgiven. I'd go as far as to say 'I know I've been forgiven'.*

*The prison system say I am to do twenty years—so be it, that's man's law, but I think my real sentence will start when I stand alone, with my Maker, and when I am told my path for my next life. I know it will be given to me with love and understanding. It's something I know not to fear. The sentence/life I will be given will be one that helps me along the path. How can you fear a soul who is pure love?* *

Although White Eagle promotes the idea of freewill in our reactions *now*, he is also careful to limit the sense of freewill inherent in what comes to us. This I think is very loving. For us to believe that we had total freewill, were that coupled with a sense of full responsibility, would be crippling. Everything that went wrong, everything we felt even remotely regretful for, would tend to assume the power of an enormous instrument of self-blame. Wisely, therefore, I think, White Eagle offers predestination as a hidden component of experience, complementing whatever can be consciously created. But this careful balance-keeping leads him to stress what our thoughts are creating *now*. This is really the main thrust of everything White Eagle says about karma: that it is better to focus on the creative power of thought now—creative for good and for ill—rather than on anything to

*For the full letter, see *Stella Polaris*, vol. 46 (1996–97), pp. 100–101.

do with the past. Thinking of it as karma is but one way of interpreting our experience, and while it can be very enlightening it is not always the most useful way; it can often distract us.

When I meditate on karma as 'action' I have the sense that White Eagle's teaching is as yet incompletely understood. The consequences of time being illusion, particularly, require much deep study. I would say that action is what we *choose* to do; and that behind this is the will. It is at that level that we need to see ourselves most clearly. Meditation on our true being enables us to invest our actions (karma) with the clarity of understanding; it enables us to own them. The actual choice we make, I suspect, is far less important than the motive behind it, the creative will. Sometimes White Eagle exhorts us to get on with doing something and not to spend too long weighing up the pros and cons. Yet paradoxically he also says, 'If in doubt, do nothing'.

The highest thing is actually to *do* right, not to know that we are doing it: another paradox, but one which returns us to our inmost awareness. The Christian idea of true spiritual poverty (*Blessed are the poor in spirit**), and the Buddhist one of non-attachment, resonate here; as does Hindu dharma, following one's good, whatever it may be. I advise further meditation!

## Using the power of thought

As to how we respond to conditions in our lives, what White Eagle advocates above all is *calmness*. That way we not only avoid creating for ourselves fresh difficulties, we also give ourselves the opportunity to create harmony instead. 'Do your best', he says; 'then you will, as you put it, shorten your karma'. But there is more to the idea than acceptance; it is the foundation of something greater. White Eagle speaks of life very helpfully in

---

*Matthew 5 : 3; compare White Eagle's teaching in THE PATH OF THE SOUL, chapter four.

terms of our building 'a soul temple'. This is a way, I think, of helping us create perfection for ourselves.

*One of the most powerful tools with which to work upon ourselves, and upon the soul temple we are all building, is thought. Although in days to come men and women will be principally concerned with the unfolding of higher or spiritual aspects of themselves, at the present time they are largely concerned with the development of the mind, the mental qualities. In spite of this, so few people take heed as to how they think; they think at random, letting their thoughts tumble and jumble along together until their minds become like rag-bags, full of all sorts of queer odds and ends. Only occasionally does one meet a mind beautifully arranged, with all its contents neatly in order and under the control of the spirit.*

*Once we begin to understand the power of thought, we can use thoughts to shape our lives to beauty and harmony.*

SPIRITUAL UNFOLDMENT 3, p. 35

White Eagle is outstanding among spiritual teachers for the amount of emphasis he places on this power we have to create harmony and beauty in our lives. As always, he relates this to service too. This is not necessarily service in a narrow sense. The highest level of service arises from such simple beginnings as the thought-control, just touched on, implies. The finer vision he gives is like that which is ascribed to the *boddhisattva* in Buddhist teaching, namely that the enlightened one cannot truly enter *nirvana* (perfection) while his or her fellow beings remain imperfect. Each of us is indeed a light for all humanity. Truly how can any of us attain happiness until everyone else is happy?

*Think of yourself as descending like a babe to this earth, in order not only to develop in yourself the qualities of the Son–Daughter of God, but in the process to help people develop and look towards the great light for their happiness and their redemption—which means their escape from the darkness of*

*lower matter, and their return to the freedom of the Sun world,
the Christ kingdom.*

SPIRITUAL UNFOLDMENT 3, pp. 50–51

No-one will want to linger when such a vision is presented.
What is the way we go about recreating our lives? First, I think,
we take charge of our thoughts. White Eagle speaks of most of
human thought as 'untidy and nebulous': he would have us recognize how that power can be enhanced, and *use it*. 'The discipline of thought-control and thought-direction is absolutely necessary to those who would become conscious of the invisible
worlds' (SPIRITUAL UNFOLDMENT 3, p. 35). While the thoughts are
uncontrolled, the life is undirected. By controlling our thoughts,
we re-establish control of our lives.

Yet White Eagle says more, namely that an ungoverned mind
is the agent of fear. The sense of his teaching is that it requires
frequent and constant re-centring of ourselves to prevent the
sloppy thought-patterns the mind so easily admits from turning
into fears that are almost self-generating. In this the symbol of
the Star is again helpful. White Eagle repeatedly follows the
Bhagavad-gita in calling the mind the 'slayer of the real': he would
have us constantly distinguish the real from the unreal, too. It is
not just the timeless as against the temporal that he implies, the
world of light as against the world of illusion; but the separation
of the world of fear from the world of trust. 'There is no need to
fear *anything*', he says, 'for even if that which you fear comes to
pass, there is always a wise and loving power which bears you up
and carries you safely over the rough places' (SPIRITUAL UNFOLD-
MENT 3, p. 40). This message is repeated many times.

## Deep fear and how it is handled

White Eagle is quick to stress that control of fear-thought is not
only good in our own lives, but important also in our attitude to

others, and most of all in healing work. We can only work as healers when our eyes are focused upon the light.

*Be careful to send forth no thoughts of fear which might well push others down the precipice of their own weakness, but rather by a constantly positive and constructive thought make yourself a rescuer. This is world service.*

SPIRITUAL UNFOLDMENT 3, p. 40

White Eagle likens negative thought to a virus which one may actually catch or transmit; positive thought, by contrast, is a shield: it is also a builder, the builder of the soul temple.

But 'positive' and 'negative' thought: what terms are these? Are we not on the edge of the same psychological issue as the one surrounding depression which I touched on in chapter three? Yes, I think up to a point we are, and the same things that apply there apply here also. Yet it is now easier to see the distinction. White Eagle speaks of us needing to be positive in our outlook, but he does not tell us to have unreasonable expectations of what life will bring. It may bring sorrow, but not sorrow without compensation. Furthermore, he acknowledges the equal power to teach that the dark and the light hold:

*You must be prepared to go through dark places as well as sunlit ones.... Do not try to escape your obligations, nor to evade the sorrows and the disappointments of human life. They come to you as opportunities.*

*We talk about good and evil. What is the difference? Both alike are teachers.*

SPIRITUAL UNFOLDMENT 4, p. 6

White Eagle's fellow guide, Silver Birch, goes further than this. He says:

*When you come to our world ... it is the dark experiences for which you will express gratitude. It is the storm and the shadow for which you will be thankful, for you will realize in your*

99

*changing viewpoint that these experiences, so unwelcome at the time, were the means by which the spirit grew. I cannot prove this to you, but you will prove it yourself one day.*

Quoted in *Psychic World*, October 1997

Clearly, there is a distinction to be made between what comes to us to teach us—even the natural sorrows that arise—and the undisciplined thought which creates unnecessarily complex conditions. White Eagle does not even say that negative thoughts are bad, simply that they are the long way round when it comes to creating centred inner happiness in our lives. He says elsewhere, 'Sometimes the soul needs pain and suffering in order to develop the deeper emotions as well as to learn to control them'.

We need both the positive and negative in our lives. Yet when it comes to what we choose now, well: because thought itself is creative, maybe we are to see the choice of the positive as simply more efficient than the choice of its opposite. The choice of sunlight demands soul effort, 'remembering' the eyes of the spirit, but deliberately making that choice certainly brings the sunlight, brings it more quickly. The negative thought brings sorrow, perhaps: but the sorry conditions are themselves teachers, bringing eventual growth, growth which leads firmly to happiness.

There is always the danger in recounting the teaching, that it becomes more and more of a challenge to live it. It may be so also with the issue of acting 'positively' or 'negatively'. I hope to have shown that when you appear to have chosen wrongly, you have not made a terrible and irreversible mistake. At any time you can recover the light by thinking back to it; there is no awful backlog to live through first. Of course, the soul that has been very immersed may find it takes a long progression of moments of remembering to do this fully, so it may feel a long path altogether: but surely this is an experience we all share?

Even among individuals who spend themselves constantly in

service, there can be an underlying feeling of hopelessness, that they are not being positive enough. That feeling may come from accumulated guilt and White Eagle would, I know, above all long to free them of it. Being in the light is a process which is just that, nothing more: no preparing to do it, no post-mortem on whether or not we have done it. It helps simply to remember the light as often as we can.

What keeps us from finding loving happiness may go very deep indeed, for all that. I quoted White Eagle as saying, 'there is no need to fear *anything*' (above, p. 98): to some this will actually seem glib, when their life-conditions seem to show precisely the opposite. What happens when the worst scenario does come to pass? How do we cope? I am afraid I cannot offer from White Eagle a solution that does not involve effort, except to reiterate that deep suffering is often what forces us to own our deepest truth. For the lucky few this may actually come spontaneously when the position is extreme. For the rest, I suggest that putting into practice the focus on the Star as a symbol of the true self is *still* the way. And those who have never known, or believe they have never known, love in their lives, may find it particularly difficult. It is like chronic pain, where a persistent calling and calling upon the power of the Star may be the only way through. Yet if what I have said is true, this love is still findable in the self, and in fact it may most easily come to the fore when we turn our attention to love of another. Here is White Eagle:

*Many of you have said to us, 'My heart is like a stone. I have not got any feeling. I cannot love'. This is not really so. It is only a crust which has to be broken through. The fire is in everyone's heart. What you will find helpful is to cultivate tolerance and patience. Try to remember the difficulties which confront the other soul, the lessons which that soul is trying to learn, the limitations which it is feeling: in other words, feel pity and tenderness, tolerance and patience. From these qualities the divine fire will rise in your heart, but first and foremost your need is to get contact with the Christ love, the love between Christ and yourself. Let the spark unite you. Get above personalities to the divine heart, and that light flowing into you will bring you warmth. You won't have the passion which earth people think is love, but something superior: a light, a gentleness, a sweetness, a kindness which without words will flow from you. That is* real *love.*

Unpublished teaching of 29th May 1946

Sometimes it is far easier to feel love for others, or for people generally, or even for animals, than it is to do anything loving to help ourselves. You will remember my little story in the Introduction, of when as a child I felt so cast down. Then, something came to me from outside (apparently) and absolutely restored my spontaneity and my happiness. In theory we should be able to do this for ourselves all the time, but I know there have been whole periods when for me 'making the contact' with the light has been really difficult. It should be possible to find the light within but the slightest feeling of guilt (or another difficult emotion) destroys for us the thought that we might have any light within us at all! What I do in those circumstances is to turn to projecting the light into the world. That way I never have to decide first whether I am a good person or not, I just get on with the service of it. I may or may not do some good to others (I trust I do!) but while I am concentrating, I make sure I stand in the light for a while myself, in my imagination. Then healing comes to me as it would to the other people I have been trying to heal; and with healing, away go my feelings of inadequacy. Sometimes finding the light is a question of tricking the limitations of our consciousness and earthly minds!

As it happens, I think the human soul is remarkably adept at finding love, though often in strange ways and sometimes at outward cost. An elderly person I knew lived most of her life without ever receiving much affection, alienated from her family and very rarely the recipient of any physical warmth. The end of her life was spent in an old people's home, where she appeared totally unable to relate to the world because of progressive senility. Yet in the warmth of care she received I know that she found something she had lacked all her life. As far as anyone on the outside can tell, I believe that at the end of her life she found a happiness different from anything she had known. That it was at such great cost is, perhaps, tragic: yet who knows what deep soul learning was done in that life, in both its phases; how resilient the soul, that the sort of path the rest of us are grateful not to tread should be its route to its own form of wellbeing?

Would that we always did convince ourselves we could find love. In the story just told I do not dwell on the pain, and I have chosen to extract the good from the situation. For quite a number of people, the same happiness is not found, and at the bottom line, suicide is the chosen way out. Personally, I find suicide one of the most difficult things to write about. In keeping with what I said earlier, I must begin by saying that every being deserves our respect regardless of what else we know about them, for in a few cases it may even be something very shocking. And suicide, very often the result of anger breaking through despair, may be a statement of rock-bottom self-respect, found beneath absolute hopelessness about what else might be done to regain respect from outside. Yet suicide in another presents our responses with one of the greatest challenges we know. White Eagle actually tells us that whatever needed to be faced has still not been faced when suicide is the choice—and it may have to be faced all over again. This *must* be heard gently, not as a further 'stick'. Comfortingly, life is continuous: the ending of it is not, in White

Eagle's teaching, quite so final as it might otherwise seem to be. Healing can take lifetimes. But it can never not happen.

So to sum up, maybe the terms 'positive' and 'negative' need not be labels by which to judge ourselves, only the field for wise advice from White Eagle. As many times as he advocates a positive outlook he also states that the positive and the negative are like the masculine and the feminine, each as important as the other in earthly life. Rather, I suspect, he asks us to remember that the whole idea of this duality is an earthly one; even if, like the illusion of time, it is a persistent one. The Buddhists would call it maya, illusion. To see with the eyes of the spirit, therefore, is not to be trenchantly positive but to stand aside from this illusion and understand that though the outworking of things uses the illusion of positive and negative aspects in life, the duality is not real. True vision sees the light within all experience, and transcends this problem altogether.

## Finding our own light

To see with the eyes of spirit is to touch, first of all, the place of the 'lighted flame' in our hearts. Spirit is love: and to find our heart-consciousness is to find the loving warmth that so quickly rises up with all the power of the Sun when we invite it in. It takes some self-control not to be dominated by our fears (and some of them are deeply hidden) but to go in absolute simplicity to this place of warmth instead. And the choice we make in this loving place, regardless of what we think, will always be *for love*: a love which we shall first of all feel in ourselves, not on behalf of anything or anyone else. Love does not exist in conforming to other people's agendas of how we should be, it actually resides in being completely open to our own spontaneity.

It is initially love for ourselves as individuals that we feel, because only by being in touch with this love can we actually offer it. We have to feel it first, and then we are a light to others! I should add that I am fully aware how much of a demand I am putting on all of us here. To set ourselves an ideal is not necessarily a bad thing, however, and what I think White Eagle does so successfully is to reinforce our belief that it is attainable. For when we truly take charge of ourselves, there is no such thing as blame of self or blame of others. Nor, ultimately, is our responsibility due to any one or any thing but our own truth. We may recognize in taking the action the desire to consider the needs of others; but we may still feel that it is kinder to them to go ahead than not to trust them with their own truth. The Society of Friends have a dictum, which is to 'live adventurously'. Like so much quoted out of context, this needs thinking about; but I think if we do so the potential for wonderful progress in improving both our own lives and those of people in general becomes apparent. Sometimes it is we that have to start by our action the movement which enables whole numbers of people to take charge of their lives, powerfully.

White Eagle, as always, sums all of this up beautifully.

*Those whose hearts are filled with love are never daunted, are not cast down; they do not give way to unworthy fears, either about themselves, their physical bodies, or the welfare of those they love, because they have been quickened by the divine light and power, and therefore nothing can go wrong. Things only go wrong when the mind of self in you starts to fret and rail against the circumstances of life, and you say, 'I am disappointed because the circumstances of life will not go as I ... I ... I want them to go!' Then suffering and chaos result, because the contact is cut. If only you had the strength to live always within the peace of God, to live in the truth—Thy will not mine!*

SPIRITUAL UNFOLDMENT 1, pp. 61–62

Our dharma, our deepest will, is the will of God.

If this is true, and I believe it is, then our deepest will holds an all-encompassing vision, a divine one. To have our thoughts centred upon God, as White Eagle advocates, is to have them set upon perfection. To give us an image of perfection to keep before us is precisely the use of the Star symbol.

Yet (for this may sound airy-fairy, overly pious even) I think it is important, and enormously freeing, to have a sense of a personal dream. It may be very mundane or short term—it may be just to complete a collection of teddy-bears—but it is ours. In the recognition of that dream, in opening ourselves to the happiness of fulfilment, we become very deeply in touch with ourselves. In any way that we can define our dream precisely, it probably falls short of perfection, because perfection is beyond the limitation of being defined. Yet behind the limited dream there is another. To look beyond, and beyond, and beyond, into a light beyond all lights, is a way to produce a most empowering fixedness of life-purpose, and it leads us to precisely the same place as any other route to clear vision I have outlined.

Whoever has this clear vision may give others some surprises in their life-choices. Yet somehow we know to respect them, for they are in touch with their own power and truth. I gave the example of Minesta and her unwavering answer to the call of spirit. There is no better clairvoyance than the focus of the inner eye upon our dream; and to go about achieving our dream keeps our vision on the light. So let us ask ourselves, with freedom— that is, with permission to hear absolutely anything that comes back to us—what our dream is. Through it, we shall know without doubt the best that we can bring ourselves and all creation by our thought-power.

CHAPTER SIX

# The Principles of the Lodge

THE IDEAS of karma and dharma form part of what are known as 'the Principles of the White Eagle Lodge'. The six Principles are the one attempt made, under White Eagle's guidance, to define a specific belief system for the Lodge. Even so, they are only intended as a guide and perhaps to stimulate thought and meditation upon deep issues. White Eagle himself is clear that they should not be taken as more than this. What he does speak of as unalterable are the spiritual laws, the definition of which forms the fifth Principle of the Lodge. He makes it clear that these laws exist whether we recognize them or not, though the way we interpret them is entirely a matter of freewill.*

Because the Principles are a *human* summary of what White Eagle teaches, the relationship between how his teaching feels in practice and how it is defined will always be slightly strained, but I believe that they remain illuminating. In this chapter, I should like to go through the Principles partly with the desire to explain what I think they mean, but also to show how meditation upon them can lead in a number of different directions,

*Angelus, October 1946, p. 213.

altogether giving a sense of the great richness of the scope of White Eagle's teaching. I shall deal in this chapter with all but the last Principle, and with that in the final chapter. Needless to say there is a historical reason for the Principles, which was to distinguish the Lodge's belief system from that of Spiritualism, whose seven Principles are differently defined. White Eagle made it clear he was happy with the six Principles as a summary, but they have certainly never been intended to be rules as to what is expected of members of the White Eagle Lodge. They are each introduced with the phrase: '*The Lodge teaches...*'.

*1) ...that God, the Eternal Spirit,*
*is both Father and Mother.*

White Eagle uses a number of different words for God, some of them from the Native American tradition, some from the Christian, others from the eastern, others even (such as 'the Great Architect') from the masonic. Occasionally he will refer separately to the great Father or the great Mother. The former is seen as the divine spirit, the bringer of life in its essence, the creator; whereas the latter, the great Mother, is the mother of life in form—thus of the world as we see it, the natural world; she is divine Mother, compassionate, the one who sees mortals both into and out of life. The Father governs human destiny, imparts the laws of life, watches wisely over the angels of karma, and ensures that all creation moves ever forward in evolution and understanding.

There is a principle of complementarity about almost all the concepts White Eagle uses. In many primitive religions there was normally a separation of the feminine God, often represented by the earth, from the masculine God, represented by the sky, and White Eagle echoes and amplifies this tradition, contrasting sun and moon, light and darkness, positive and negative, giving and receiving, the reasoning mind and the receptive mind or feelings, and so on.

It is arguable that the sense of vitality within these pairs of opposites has been lost in modern life, where the masculine aspects have been extended at the expense of the feminine. White Eagle never criticizes any other religion or teacher, such as one that countenances only a male God, but he would point to all the attributes of the Mother and ask us if we could conceive of life, or indeed conceive life, without her. In one talk, he spoke of the time in history when humanity's once-female deities were rejected for male ones. In the earliest times, people recognized in woman

*a demonstration of the continuity of life, so they worshipped the Mother as God–Creator. Later on men said that they were made in the image of God, and God was therefore a man, and woman was not then regarded with veneration. [But] the ancients ... worshipped the giver of life as the great Mother. A mother ... has an antidote for her child's suffering. A mother has wisdom in guiding the tottering steps. The great Mother was therefore the adored one.*

Unpublished teaching of 20th July 1954

In an article on the six Principles Joan Hodgson uses the concept of angels as creators of form to explain the role of divine Mother in the scheme of things:

*The creation of bodies and nurture of souls is the province of the divine Mother aspect of God, the divine Mother who creates ever new and more perfect forms through which the spirit can manifest. She has at her command the angels of form, the angels who are responsible for the creation of all the life-forms in the nature kingdom, and for the evolution of the soul from the animal to the human to the divine state.*

*Stella Polaris*, vol. 40 (1990–91), p. 18

Also, one might add, for the evolution of the seed into the plant, for the creation and recreation of the seas and mountains, for the balance of life in the natural world: for the earth herself. We shall extend this concept in the next Principle.

*2) ...that the Son, the Cosmic Christ, is also the light which shines in the human heart. By reason of this divine sonship, all are brothers and sisters in spirit, a brotherhood which embraces all life visible and invisible, including the fairy and angelic kingdoms.*

White Eagle's teaching about the divine Son, and how he means more than the earthly being of Jesus when he refers to the Son, is something to which I have already alluded, in relation to healing. The concept of the Christ is not a specifically male one. White Eagle often refers to the divine Son–Daughter. At other times he makes a play on the pronunciation in English that this word 'Son' and the 'Sun' share, to the extent that sometimes when reading transcripts of his teaching it is difficult to know which of them he meant. This seems quite deliberate. He ascribes power to the physical sun almost with the passion of a sun-worshipper of old, yet he makes what he calls 'the spiritual Sun' or 'Christ Sun' all the more powerful still. Sometimes he describes the latter as being 'behind the physical sun'. I hasten to add that this is not meant literally, though I once had a hard time explaining to an enquirer that it was not! Yet to say that the power of the spiritual Sun shines through the physical one is wholly consonant with White Eagle's teaching.

More than this, though, White Eagle gives a form to the spiritual Sun, and so makes it almost a being in itself.

*A great being uses the Sun as his–her vehicle for distributing life to the universe. May these angels be real to you; may you work and live in harmony with them.*

Unpublished teaching of 15th February 1937

Picturing a flame within, or a tiny Star of light, is the most convenient way to conceive of the indwelling Son or Sun. In truth all life is spirit, all creation emanates from the Father–Mother God. Thus in a sense, the Son is all of life, and all of creation is illumined by the light of the spiritual Sun. This is the key to understanding the concept of the universal brotherhood of life. There are some mysteries here, and they do require meditation; the finite mind cannot grasp everything. How can the earth be all light when so clearly to our ordinary senses much of it is full of darkness, evil? First, White Eagle would say, because every individual soul is nonetheless at all times seeking the light, however tortuously. The deeds they do, perhaps in the mistaken hope of finding truth, may be evil, but the souls themselves are still on the same path as the rest of us. And who knows what we, too, unwittingly do—or how much, even at the moments in our lives we regard with horror, we are actually seeking light? Yet the spirit angle on this is unequivocal, that darkness is illusion: all is *one*, there is no real duality. Darkness, however real it may appear, is only where there *seems* to be no light. Light is everywhere, it is just that we cannot see it. (What was said earlier about 'positive' and 'negative' can be reiterated here: *that* duality, too, is unreal.) It is probably best to recall that the overriding principle is love, and then it is not so difficult to understand the message I believe White Eagle wishes to convey, which is that both dark and light are used by spirit to bring us home.

There is also a little confusion about 'Son' and 'Sun' in the foregoing which is worth explaining for the sake of the alert reader who has noticed it! As the first two Lodge Principles suggest, White Eagle conceives of a trinity redefined as Father, Mother, Son. There is not too much discrepancy from the orthodox here, for even within the Christian tradition the three aspects of the trinity are often regarded as containing each other:

what White Eagle redefines are the parts, not the whole! However, when it comes to the physical sun, he often uses this as an image of the Father-principle, with the moon representing the Mother. This association is traditional, of course, and it is fine until he also makes the connection mentioned earlier between 'Sun' and 'Son'. He thus seems to imply that the physical sun stands for both the Father and the Son in the trinity!

What he means, I think, is that in the way in which we look to the sun as the source of life, we are looking upwards to the Father, the Creator. Yet when we think of what is created, this has to embrace the whole universe, including the physical sun; and so when White Eagle uses 'Sun' and 'Son' interchangeably he is speaking of the whole relationship between creator and created, Father and Son, and there is no better symbol for this than the sun in the sky. *I and my Father are one*, said Jesus: the mystery that creator and created are the same may lead to all sorts of interesting semantics if we want them to, and yet the power of this mystical concept, not exclusive to White Eagle, is without price.

His term, 'the Cosmic Christ', is moreover helpful in this problem. In the first passage quoted in this section, he says that the physical sun has a spiritual counterpart which is the embodiment of the divine in a form which we can recognize. This is the Cosmic Christ. It is the coming of that being into a human form which is represented by the incarnation of Jesus, the Christ.

*The Cosmic Christ is not only a radiation, a power unseen and too often unfelt; it has form, a human form. We do not say that the whole radiation of the spiritual emanation from the Sun can be confined to one human form; we say that it can manifest in great power through a perfectly beautiful human form.*

THE WAY OF THE SUN, p. 43

Seen from an earthly viewpoint, 'the Cosmic Christ' seems so far above us, so far even above the personality of Jesus in whom the Christ was incarnated, as to be almost beyond conception. Seen, though, from the opposite perspective, the descent of the Cosmic Christ into the simplest human form—that of the child, the babe in the manger—is a symbol of the greatest beauty.

One might say that the Cosmic Christ is both the point at which the formless takes form, and the point at which form as we know it ceases to be distinguishable from the Oneness. Our six-pointed Star symbol is with us again. The coming together of the downward-pointing and upward-pointing triangles which make up the six-pointed Star may be the best metaphor for this concept: it describes, in other words, the point at which form and non-form meet. Once again, the real key to understanding lies in the imagination, not in the rational mind. To dwell *imaginatively* upon the concept of the Cosmic Christ offers none of the difficulty that is involved in grasping it intellectually. The passage in THE WAY OF THE SUN quoted above is followed shortly after by this one (p. 44):

*We would like you to conceive the perfect human form of the Cosmic Christ, or Christ the lord of earth's humanity, surrounded by his–her younger brethren, who are part of his–her spirit, all part of the spirit of the whole—all brethren of the same spirit.*

This quotation moves us on to another element of the second Principle, namely the brotherhood of all life. The word 'brotherhood' denotes an attitude, indeed rather more than that, an unalterable link between all forms of life. This meaning will be clear from the way in which it is used both here and elsewhere in White Eagle's teaching. The limitations of the actual word have to be acknowledged, for heard with horse-sense it sounds like a group of men coming together in community. Yet 'sisterhood' (as an alternative) has a meaning which is really only gender-specific and in normal usage does not have the broader sense that the concept demands. The Lodge prefers to live with this problem rather than come up with alternatives that are unwieldy, for it is no stranger anyway to the limitations of language!

To state it categorically, though, let me say that 'brotherhood' is meant to be totally nonspecific and to refer not only to every member of the human race but additionally to the creatures, the plants, the components of the natural world, and even the planets and stars. Most significantly, brotherhood is seen to extend beyond the physical world and to include all those in spirit and other streams of life. 'Brother–sisterhood' would still be exclusive of the other forms of life. Maybe as the English language unfolds, a more obviously comprehensive term will emerge.

Some readers may be surprised at how the composition of this brotherhood is denoted in the Principle: the phrase 'the fairy and angelic kingdoms' will come across easily to some, with difficulty to others. I will try to explain. White Eagle, as one would expect from someone of the Native American tradition, sees all life as animate, living. He speaks of a lifestream different from our own which exists in the rocks and stones, the plants; the fire, water, air and earth. He describes this as the 'angelic' or 'elemental' lifestream. To my mind the easiest way to understand the concept is to regard the whole of life as continuous creation, and to suppose that the very smallest agents of creation are themselves animate: little sparks of the creative energy, but every one of them alive, conscious, I suppose one might say. To describe this idea in terms of popular mythology—that is, a hierarchy of little beings, commonly called fairies—perhaps takes a discarnate being a certain courage! And ultimately words are unnecessary: the *principle* is that all creation is alive, and that in the onward process of creation the very agents of growth and movement are alive too. These are the 'spirits', the angels, the devic beings: they are nature *alive*.

At the same time, White Eagle does call them 'a separate line of evolution' and this concept has to be understood if in turn we are fully to understand his teaching. The phrase implies that these very beings evolve further. What they evolve from and to may be beyond our comprehension, but White Eagle identifies all sorts of orders and types. There are the spirits active in the blooming of a flower, and in the great span of years an oak tree lasts; there are the angelic beings involved in the execution of divine law, such as karma, and in guarding and looking after us—our guardian angels—and those who preside over birth and death.

Along with the Theosophists, White Eagle speaks of the seven great rays of evolution, each with an angelic being at their head; and at times he also refers to astrological symbols in angelic terms: the planetary angels, the angels of Venus, and so on. He equates the first three of the rays of evolution with the three aspects of the trinity, using both the names of the Father–Mother–Son and the attribute names, those respectively of power (or will), love (altruism) and wisdom (philosophy). The fourth ray is that of harmony, the fifth knowledge or science, the sixth devotion, and the seventh ceremonial magic. The last three form a second allusion to the trinity, in that they too correspond respectively to wisdom, love and power. Nicely, the fourth can be seen as a pivotal point, joining the two triangles, which is entirely in keeping with its quality of harmony. Of these seven rays, it is the second (love), the sixth (devotion), and the seventh (ceremonial magic) that are reckoned to be most associated with the Lodge itself. The seven rays tie in with an astrological map of the cosmos, as well as a Theosophical one.

White Eagle's SPIRITUAL UNFOLDMENT 2 is the best source-book for all his teaching on the inner life within nature and in the wider universe, although a further book about angels is also being compiled at New Lands from his teaching as I write.

I should like to free the reader a little at this point, by admitting the freedom I give myself. To me the aspect of White Eagle's teaching that most appeals is the way in which we are led to find the Oneness within ourselves through meditation and communion. The complex picture of the Oneness as a great kaleidoscope of beings offers great possibilities, but for me it is less rewarding than seeing life as an undifferentiated whole. At the same time I have to acknowledge that a kaleidoscopic pattern is generally beautiful, and that the concept of the varied brotherhood of life, *visible and invisible*, is infinitely more beautiful than that.

If we choose to see creation in the kaleidoscopic way, White Eagle helps us to see yet more patterns and symmetries. There is not only the seven-ray system, but the imprint of the twelve-sign zodiac too; there are all the separate levels of the angelic hierarchy. We can, if we wish, study all the different 'planes' of life, which White Eagle states most simply as being the physical, astral, mental, and celestial, but which may be given in a rather more complex way.* I have to admit that in their own way these patterns and structures reflect a complexity in life that is amply borne out by what we know of our physical universe: the complex chemical structures modern medicine entails would be one random example, or the mathematical and physical constructs which end in our ability to put spacecraft on the surface of Mars or send them to Saturn. The human mind grasps all this excellently; it also handles the complex structures of language. I think there is a part of me that loves a Quaker simplicity, though!— and finds silence often preferable to a lot of discussion. The happy truth is that we can choose. All of us, at one time or another, will tend to have a thirst for complexity, or for simplicity. My re-

*See ARTHUR CONAN DOYLE'S BOOK OF THE BEYOND, especially pp. 45–46.

marks are intended to be permissive, that is to allow the reader to feel he or she may take these hierarchies on board or not as a matter of choice. So long as we retain the power of choice none of the things I have described will worry us one way or another. And do the 'eyes of the spirit' choose? I suspect that they can at one and the same time see life as infinitely varied and complex, just as we ourselves are; and at others, see both it and us as of utter simplicity. White Eagle speaks of the great masters at the head of each ray of life, but he also tells us that from the level of spirit, they are so close to one another as to be almost indistinguishable. To hold to simplicity, while at the same time giving imaginative sympathy to the more complex view of life's hierarchies, enables us to give intense value to life through ceremony and festival, and ritual. We can see the whole within the detail, and we can notice the detail within the whole. White Eagle has deep and rich teaching, some of it in THE WAY OF THE SUN, about the meaning of the festivals of the year, both the Christian festivals and some of the others: the Buddhist Wesak festival, for instance, and the rituals associated with sowing and harvest, and the festival of Remembrance, which he identifies as far, far older than the twentieth-century version associated with war.

*3) ...the expression of these Principles in daily life through service.*

It is interesting that this Principle is included after two which between them describe the trinity of Father–Mother–Son, and the brotherhood of all life. What we therefore express through service is the God within us in all its forms: in the simplest sense, we allow the light within us to shine, and the service which we offer life is at its heart simply to be ourselves, to *be* God to the fullest degree.* To live consciously is service; and to serve is to be absolutely true to all of life.

Choosing a conscious form of service provides, additionally, an opportunity to open the heart through compassion. Compassion comes when we recognize other people's or other creatures' suffering in our own hearts. Taken on willingly, a life of service offers all sorts of opportunities for growth that a life of seeking self in isolation does not, even though the latter may outwardly offer more freedom. White Eagle says that only in conscious engagement with the lives of others, in other words in brotherhood, can the soul find full illumination. Self-isolation, for instance in long meditation, brings understanding only up to a point. But he acknowledged to a questioner: 'If the service is given automatically, it would not be very lovely, but if performed with the thought of giving the other something to help him or her spiritually, then you contribute a higher form of love'.† Creativity and imagination seem to be keywords beneath this, if we listen carefully. Thus a life of service in the old-fashioned sense of the word might not be very useful if done by rote: it could even be undertaken out of reluctant duty or self-punishment and thus go right against the deeper self (though I think at the very last analysis the self knows its own need).

*This above all: to thine own self be true.* It has often been suggested that this saying, from Shakespeare, has its origin in the inner mystical tradition. It is inwardly that we are most free and White Eagle seeks to remind us of this many times.

There is a specific form of service offered in White Eagle's work, which allows the feelings we may have for brotherhood with all life to be used in an active and organized way. The White Eagle Star Brotherhood meet at regular times and focus clearly upon the six-pointed Star. That Star reminds us of things being raised to perfection: the human raised to perfect health, global

*This suggestion is beautifully backed up by PRAYER IN THE NEW AGE, p. 31.
†Unpublished teaching of 29th May 1946.

political situations working out perfectly, environmental challenges met, and all brought into perfect harmony and balance. Through focus on the Star and the simple calling of the name of any person, place or country that needs healing, that person or condition is seen in perfect, rather than in disordered, manifestation. Another way to see how this works may be as sympathetic vibration: our calling upon the power of the Star causes a vibration to go forth from it which in turn stimulates certain vibrations in life itself. The creative power of thought is thus used to bring harmony to situations and individuals.

Anyone may participate in this work, which I have already touched upon in chapter four. White Eagle makes the suggestion that we endeavour to 'send forth the Light' at the hours of 3.00, 6.00, 9.00 and 12.00 (there are more details of this, and of the recently-conceived White Eagle Star Link, in the Appendix, pp. 160, 163–64). Through training in the use of the Star we come to see it as a more and more powerful symbol. It becomes absolutely real to us, and the balance which it conveys leads us to a deep equilibrium in ourselves. This is not a moral quality we might claim, but rather something within us which we can find ever more easily. The Star Brotherhood of the Lodge is for those who wish to make an even deeper commitment to this idea or ideal. Its work is the core and indeed the origin too of the whole Lodge work. It is through its silent devotion and meditation that the vision of the Lodge is held.

The healing service offered for individuals (and also for animals), which extends the work with the Star, is historically an aspect of this Brotherhood work, and it generally forms part of the training for that work. All such service is voluntary.

Healing is service, understanding is service, study of nature and its laws is service, living our lives is service. Service comes from the natural desire of the human heart.

It is no surprise that White Eagle's teaching has been called 'A Religion of Happiness': to be happy is itself to serve life. Yet God is more (one feels) than a passive expression of happiness within earthly life. The God within is an active caring, a loving of all life, an understanding. At the end of the little book THE QUIET MIND (p. 96) is White Eagle's saying:

> Happiness is the realization of God in the heart. Happiness is the result of praise and thanksgiving, of faith, of acceptance; a quiet, tranquil realization of the love of God. This brings to the soul perfect and indescribable happiness. God is happiness.

*4) ...the awareness of the invisible world, which bridges separation and death and reveals the eternal unity of life.*

All life is spirit: I have sought to show that this is the central tenet of White Eagle's teaching. We might say that in his teaching traditional Spiritualism is replaced with a true spiritualism where the oneness of all life rather than the continuity of it is paramount. Yet White Eagle does clearly speak of the benefit of developing clear vision. For some this means simply seeing onto the level of life just above the physical, where things in nature seem to have an additional shimmer of light and energy to them, and where those thought of as 'dead' can, with a little training on the part of the watcher, be glimpsed. For others, there exists the wonderful ability to look into the life-experience with the clarity of the true medium. All worlds truly are one: the key to finding this is to look at them not with limited earthly eyes but with the eyes of the spirit.

Allowing the consciousness to work from the heart, allowing the earthly eyes to soften their focus slightly, and yet looking with brightness and intensity at the natural world, may enable any one of us to see the life within nature more clearly. This is worth trying as an exercise in itself. White Eagle described a more specific technique in the quotation made on p. 24. More helpful still is an extended meditation in which, after we have entered into communion at the highest level of life, we can then see onto all planes of life. Most of us require long practice to do this! In this exalted condition of awareness there really is no separation between us and souls who have left physical life, nor is there any consciousness of separation between ourselves and others in this life—all isolation is illusion.

Any sort of training in clairvoyance may seem either exciting, or daunting, or both. The secret, from my own experience, is simply to be quiet and trusting and *allow* whatever we think we may see to be real. If it feels good, and loving, then let us allow it to be true: not with the mind, but creatively. The clairvoyant vision is much more accessible in most of us than we think, and there is no reason why in some cases it cannot be quite spontaneous. Very often, it is a matter of not mistrusting it, not killing it off, rather than hard work spent in developing it.

White Eagle teaches that there is more to clairvoyance than seeing into the realms beyond death to make a contact there. As well as revealing to us intense beauties in nature quite invisible to the physical eye, the development of clear vision brings to us a better understanding of ourselves and other people and the reasons we act as we do. It takes us, truly, onto a higher plane of consciousness on which we have much more imaginative grasp of motives and needs, or of the individual destiny. There is thus a real increase in awareness and a real knowing, something the use of a physical medium can never bring us. Minesta's own gift, which I described in the first chapter (in particular on p. 23), had elements of this in it, and it was the sort of clairvoyance she truly wished to encourage. 'To know all is to forgive all' is an old saying; to see clearly into human life is not only to be in a position to forgive it but to love it as well. As our consciousness grows we see beauty in things which never before seemed to be beautiful. Or is it that by making the inner contact as we see them, we ourselves endow them with beauty?

This leads us to a final thought, not so much stated as implied, I think, in White Eagle's teaching. As I understand him, White Eagle says that the purpose of incarnation is that we may take the light of being into unevolved matter or chaos (*The light shineth in darkness; and the darkness comprehended it not*, John 1 : 5). Would it be true to say that one of his greatest instructions to us is to reclaim, imaginatively, everything in life that seems to be unevolved; and, through training of our own eyes, and through training of our thoughts, both see and make it beautiful? In other words, like the artist who sees beauty in many things that the average eye misses, our purpose is to bring love into all things, however dark, individually, they may seem. Here is a hint from a very early White Eagle teaching that this may be true.

*You live in a world both beautiful and ugly.... Why does the world seem ugly, why seem its people ugly? Why is the world beautiful, and why seem its people beautiful to you? When the Light Divine enters your heart, then the world becomes beautiful, and all ugliness disappears.*

Unpublished teaching of 6th May 1934

To extend our love, or our sense of beauty (I do not here separate them) to something traditionally unloved or unbeautiful may then be a way of allowing 'the Light Divine' into our hearts. You may recall the words quoted in the previous chapter from one of White Eagle's prayers: 'Yes, even in that which appears to be unenlightened, may we see the beauty of thy work' (PRAYER IN THE NEW AGE, p. 31). Our task is, in other words, creative. We are, through our onward evolution and unfoldment, co-creators with God.

Do we fully realize just how powerful a thing it is when we raise our consciousness?

*5) ...that life is governed by the five cosmic laws*
—*Reincarnation*
—*Cause and effect, or karma*
—*Opportunity*
—*Correspondences*
—*Compensation (equilibrium and balance).*

## Reincarnation, Cause and effect, and Opportunity

The first three of these so-called 'cosmic laws' have already been spoken of extensively in the chapter about the creative power of thought (chapter five). One of the points I made there was how our sense of linear time narrows our understanding of karma, and what White Eagle's teaching does to help us round this problem. It is interesting that on the subject of something so fundamental to White Eagle's teaching as reincarnation—something he actually describes as a 'law'—he sounds a similar warning about taking the idea too simplistically. It may shock a few readers if I quote him as saying, in an early talk, 'Reincarnation as usually understood is an illusion' (23rd September 1936).

How can he make a statement so apparently counter to the rest of his teaching as that? Well, actually I think it is wholly in keeping with his teaching, because it forces us to understand it at the heart level, not the intellectual. He says in the same talk: 'It is impossible to convey in earth language the inner mysteries of life'. What he helps us to understand in this teaching is that reincarnation as generally presented ties us to a notion of separateness. Conventionally, we are man Y or woman Y in this life; in the previous one, we were man or woman X, and in the one to come we will be man or woman Z. 'You like to have all your 't's crossed and your 'i's dotted', he says, but in fact 'immediately you cling to a personality, to a particular person, you lose the real meaning of what you are'.

Individuality, he goes on to say, is something that the mind takes us into. It is the mind's job as we reincarnate to take us more deeply into separateness, at least for a while. Yet the moment our individualization gets to a certain point, the soul desires identification with the whole, and starts to lose that very sense of separateness: something I suspect we all find, up to a point, even in our present incarnation—we begin to identify more with *all* life. So the sense of being separate is all the mind's work: we are in that one sense separate—just to the extent that the mind tells us, no more and no less—but really this is illusion.

How does this apply to reincarnation? Well, one thing that does come across from closely reading the talk mentioned is that the reason so many of us identify with great figures in history is that the great being behind these characters is of such force that it admits of almost a ray of life in itself. We actually *have*, in part, incarnated as that character, but within their lifestream, and not to the exclusion of other souls doing so.

I think this is extraordinarily difficult for the mind to grasp without it going into endless further speculation (but perhaps the heart finds it easy?). White Eagle actually uses it as a way to remind us of our own vastness, though, once the cloak of our individuality is removed. From the same teaching:

*Not solely are you John Smith, but a great soul impulse, which is being individualized and grows into the fullness of a perfect God-life. Behind all this there is something so grand and beautiful, that all the little pettinesses and smallnesses of personality fade into insignificance.*

To me, reincarnation is a useful idea because it takes us away from the narrow blinkers that could well make us regard our lives as futile. It provides *a way of looking at our experience* and at the same time helps to explain a number of remarkable experiences of recall that people have had which are otherwise far more difficult, if impossible, to explain. Such things are tremendously real for many of us, including myself. However, though White Eagle normally assumes that we accept the idea of reincarnation in one form or another, he does not concentrate on it to the exclusion of other ways of looking at life.

Let us for a moment assume that the alternative idea is the true one, namely that we only live once. Holding this, we may well feel that so much has to be learnt and achieved that we are likely to die long before we attain to all we need to know. So what is the point of our life? Religions have offered many possible answers to this question—arguably it is the central question which arises in any religion which conceives of life as one short span—and in orthodox Christianity the answers do bring about a strong and useful focus on *this* life. The focal point of discussion tends to be the being of Jesus, whose dying for our sins is seen as removing the necessity for every nook or cranny of experience to be explored by every individual soul. It thus provides a completeness our lives would otherwise lack. Personally, I prefer to see us doing our own work of salvation through discovery of the Christ within over many incarnations. White Eagle actually puts it in a more comforting way than that: the Christ within us, which we learn to recognize, actually saves us. Since I was brought up to take reincarnation as a law of life, it is quite difficult for me to see life in any other way than one in which 'salvation' (without the heavy weight that is so often attached to it in Christianity) is achieved through slow inner realization— the Gnostic way, in effect. The following inspiring words of White Eagle's are some I have more or less committed to memory.

*Be true to your own self, your own spirit, and in being true to yourself you will be true also to God and the universal brotherhood. Practise this daily realization of the great white light within your own being and project it forth into the world. Then, my friends, the mists around the earth will gradually be dispelled.*

*Do not look to others to do the work for you. Everyone is their own saviour, and every one of you is the saviour of all human kind.*

PRAYER IN THE NEW AGE, pp. 45–46

Far be it from me, though, to insist to those less naturally inclined to belief in reincarnation that it is the only way. I do not think White Eagle would ever do this. If forced to limit my belief system to one idea only, it would be that love is at the heart of everything. At times I feel that life is not to be defined in this or that way: that to hold to no belief too rigidly is by far the most freeing thing. If so, my first assumption—and it is one that the White Eagle teaching I quoted at the start of this section positively invites—is one of infinite possibility. Reincarnation may not be the only idea that helps us understand life. All White Eagle ever says categorically is that life is consciousness. To focus entirely and absolutely on existence now, without the conceptual distraction of another life, can often be hugely helpful.

Most of our problems arise, I suspect, when we expect to do too much with our minds and not enough with our imagination. As the reader will by now be well aware, I prefer a sense of open possibility to a defined system. Exactly the sense of infinite possibility that I find so helpful is inherent in the following brief passage from White Eagle's teaching, for it does not limit our consciousness to an earthly body, but explores a wider concept. Do human beings really have the boundaries surrounding their consciousness that we conventionally believe? Here, the phrase he is trying to define is 'matter which is conscious'.

*That [phrase] will perhaps be difficult for you to understand,*
*but we repeat, matter which is conscious, which has conscious-*
*ness, and an earth which breathes. Yes, the earth breathes,*
*otherwise it would not continue to live. The earth breathes in*
*God's love, breathes out life. Each one of you lives and has*
*your being in this same infinite consciousness. Therefore all*
*physical matter is but a condition of consciousness. The in-*
*animate is yet alive, for there is no such thing as death.*

Unpublished teaching of 6th May 1934

A consciousness continuous throughout life—what a concept!

## Correspondences and Compensation (equilibrium and balance)

The two remaining laws  probably require a little of the expanded
awareness the foregoing passage demands, too, in order to understand them. In a sense all of these 'great laws' have, for me,
the characteristic of something we barely understand, because
our power to conceive of them is insufficiently developed. Here,
however, is White Eagle speaking of the first of the two remaining laws, sometimes called the law of harmony:

*It is the law by which the human soul reflects itself upon the*
*finer ethers, upon the astral plane of desires and emotions.*
*The conditions on the astral, the mental and the spiritual planes*
*are the soul reflections which the soul's life on earth throws*
*upon the invisible planes; 'As above, so below; as below, so*
*above'. Therefore, when the soul seeks divine illumination and*
*endeavours to express the qualities of God, it is reflecting the*
*heavenly into everyday life. You cannot fail to recognize the*
*saint or elder sister–brother, because the light within such a*
*one is a reflection from the heavens. Like always reflects like.*

From the booklet *The Five Great Laws*, p. 5

This final comment, in effect saying 'it takes one to know one', carries its own profundity and encouragement. It has often seemed to me that when we admire people—whether in history or among our contemporaries—the identification of the qualities we admire in them is the clearest guide to our own ideals. Maybe what they touch in us is our own capacity, perhaps hardly acknowledged, to emulate them? Does our personal dream already exist in us? Maybe if we credited ourselves with our own ideals we would find that we actually have more of the perfect being in us than we generally think?

My aunt Joan Hodgson wrote quite extensively about the five great laws, and not least in her book WHY ON EARTH; and it is one of the best tributes I can pay to her work on them to quote something she wrote on this law. She said (pp. 41–42) that it

*implies a peculiarly close relationship between man–woman the microcosm, and God the macrocosm. We can only begin to understand it when we realize that all outer and visible manifestation is the result of an inner and invisible will or creative urge; in other words, of thought. The whole manifested universe is the result of God's thought, and man–woman, made in God's image, possesses in embryo God's creative powers. The individual is itself a God in the making.*

*The law of Correspondences is also a law of externalization, whereby the state of our inner consciousness gradually and inevitably externalizes itself in the physical body....*

She goes on to show how this law is the key to understanding the theoretical basis of disciplines like astrology, diagnosis of illness from signs which manifest in characteristics of the external body, the psychological study of handwriting, and so on. Much of her work might be described as an amplification of the law of correspondences; one of her favourite quotations, a perfect exposition of this law, was the one written over the doors of the temples of the mysteries: 'Man, know thyself: and thou shalt know God and the Universe'.

For the law of compensation or equilibrium, I return to White Eagle's own words for a defining statement, namely that it is 'the law of perfect balance and supreme justice'.

*We have said on previous occasions that there is no such thing as innocent suffering. Nevertheless you will see many instances which affront your sense of justice, and will cite many cases in which the innocent appear to suffer. Perhaps souls which seem to suffer unjustly are being presented with an opportunity for soul growth, about which you know nothing? May they not have earned such an opportunity by good action in the past?... Although this or that soul may apparently suffer injustice, by its reaction it may learn important and vital truths, which will bring happiness and blessing and expansion of consciousness to the soul. So it is as well for us all to recognize the law of equilibrium as the law of absolute and perfect justice for human life, the balancing of all apparent injustice and pain with corresponding happiness.*

*The Five Great Laws*, pp. 5–6

Conceiving of life being governed by universal law involves a wholly different way of looking at it from the conventional western one. We are used to thinking of law as being something external, and of accepted morality as being the basis of most law. It is conspicuous that the laws White Eagle defines are not tied to moral teaching: but spiritual law is not to be limited by human concerns. We may individually want to draw a personal sense of morality into the law of karma but, as White Eagle says, no-one else judges us; the only judgment is the one we make upon ourselves when the life is complete. Very reassuringly—and typically so—what White Eagle says is that 'As soon as you have learnt the lesson your karma is meant to teach you, it will fall away, it will no longer exist'.* What is most noticeable about these laws is how very closely they relate to each other; they do give a sense of overall consistency, of completeness, even though as a system they seem stripped down to essentials as a way of understanding the outworking of the divine in human life.

In the way that they come together they all add up to one thing. Just as Jesus summed up the ten commandments of Moses into two only, so White Eagle would say quite simply that there is only one law. That law, of course, is the law of love, and it is just the same as those two commandments, one of them being to love God with every atom of our being, and the other to love (is that just to recognize Him–Her in?) every created being. It is a law that we can break, and indeed we do so, again and again; but White Eagle would absolutely reassure us that so perfect is life, to transgress is simply to open ourselves to the learning of a lesson. To break the law is itself all accounted for in the great plan of life. To be in this so-called imperfect world really does involve us in a battle against fear in which, every time we give in, it goes against the law of love. But every seeming lapse is a dis-covery for us: in the discovery of what to be away from love is like, we are forced—beautifully so—to bring, ultimately, and maybe by slow means such as illness, our love into the situation. We learn through love.

The five great laws are best understood as the way to under-stand this process.

*Quoted in *Stella Polaris*, vol. 45 (1995–96), p. 138.

CHAPTER SEVEN

# The Lodge ideals and vision: the sixth Principle

SO FAR I have touched upon brotherhood as an ideal of community, in the abstract sense and as a group of people who meet to send out the light, although I did add to this the idea that brotherhood extends throughout all creation. In discussing the final Principle, it is necessary to look a little more at the history surrounding the term 'brotherhood' and at its abstract meanings. Here is the sixth Principle itself. *The Lodge teaches...*

*... that the ultimate goal of human kind is that the inner light should become so strong and radiant that even the cells of the physical body are transmuted into finer substances which can overcome mortality. This is known as the Christing of man–woman, or (in the words of the ancient Brotherhood) the blooming of the Rose on the Cross of matter.*

The image of the rose and the cross is part of the legacy of the Rosicrucian (rosy cross) brotherhood, which historically was founded by Christian Rosenkreutz in the thirteenth century but which was revived and reached a high point of popularity in the seventeenth and eighteenth centuries. (It would be incorrect to note any allusion to more modern Rosicrucianism.) White Eagle says this brotherhood is real and that it exists both sides of death. The brotherhood, in its true form, is older than Rosicrucianism. White Eagle would say that in one sense or another it dates from the beginning of time. What might seem to be an abstract notion—that all creation is linked in brotherhood—he chooses to make much more specific, stating that there is a conscious brotherhood existing between beings from time immemorial.

The history of the idea now becomes less important than the idealistic vision offered by Rosicrucianism, namely 'the blooming of the Rose on the Cross of matter'. The idea requires some explanation. In the first place, it implies an eventual joy that comes out of suffering. Human incarnation (the cross) leads to illumination (the rose). It probably helps to give this idea full emotional depth by comparing it with the *consolamentum*\* of the Albigenses or Cathars. This was the mystical revelation to be found or achieved by the seeker, a vision into the inner world, and one of utter and irreversible consolation and upliftment.

'The blooming of the Rose' has all this sense of finding absolute peace and enlightenment. It owes something to the medieval mystical vision of Christ's cross as a living tree which could miraculously bloom. But the blooming of the cross is an icon of the resurrection, and thus what is implicit in this phrase is that the human being, the individual soul, can by the example of the Christ itself reach the level at which it can resurrect itself, overcome death. Again, this idea is not intended to be limitedly 'Christian', doctrinally. Such an idea opens us to the full implication of the soul's perfectibility through the course of human incarnation. The rose is perfection through experience.

\*Readers to whom this term is unknown are directed to ARTHUR CONAN DOYLE'S BOOK OF THE BEYOND, pp. 143–49.

The salvation or perfection of the individual soul, what Indian philosophy would call the *atman*, is something unique to that soul. Its experience is utterly personal, and no priest or intercessor can do it for any man or woman: the saving power is the Christ within each of us. You will remember perhaps the sentence 'Everyone is their own saviour, and every one of you is the saviour of all humanity', which I quoted.

To catch this distinction from orthodoxy, to recognize how White Eagle sees every soul finding its own inner salvation (an idea more Gnostic than orthodox) is the key to understanding something people periodically ask about: namely why the term 'Lodge' is used in preference to 'Church'. Although it is not unreasonable to use the word 'church' in describing the Lodge, the term will never fit very exactly. The symbol of the 'church' in the Christian tradition is that the organization itself—albeit composed entirely of its members and nothing else—is 'the bride of Christ': wedded to the Christ and thus mystically become one. The image at the heart of the Lodge is rather that through the development of true brotherhood in the heart of each individual, the being within is truly realized and therefore the Christ-spirit shines forth from within.

In White Eagle's teaching, every man, woman and child is to be seen as unrealized Christ. The sixth Principle attempts to express how the unrealized becomes realized.

'The development of true brotherhood in the heart': this is an ideal which demands more than mere lip-service to an attractive, but supposedly unattainable, concept like human perfectibility. It is a central goal to be won through life, because physical life is the only way in which we can win it. One might say that the only way in which we can fully discover our brotherhood with the rest of life is by first forgetting—at birth—the love that links us all and then, through seeing what its absence looks like, rediscovering it. How this discovery must feel for us, when fully attained, is not easy to imagine. St Paul's words, *Eye hath not seen, nor ear heard … the things which God hath prepared for them that love him;* or what Jesus said to the thief crucified alongside him, *Today shalt thou be with me in paradise*: these give a clue or promise.* We for an instant rediscover the intensity of the joy of universal brotherhood on occasions such as the spontaneous moment of forgiveness when humour supersedes condemnation; in moments when our hearts suddenly melt at another person's act of kindness; through the experience of being in love, and so on. All these are times when mental control collapses and the simple responses of the heart take over.

I take another little point from history: many years ago the Lodge inherited from the Polaire Brotherhood a specific 'Rule', like a monastic rule.† The elements in this Rule included the avoidance of binding dogma, abstention from political conflict, the setting aside of personal ambition, the overcoming of egotism, the awareness that 'truth lies in the spirit', respect of women by men and general sobriety of life, respect for the animal world, the setting of an example through the Polaire ideals, and the idea that the Polaire was primarily a citizen of 'a world wherein all are to him or her brethren, but also a loving son or daughter of his or her own country'. These were the public aspects. Inwardly, the Polaire undertook never to enter the inner place (the sanctuary, or the heart itself) bearing anger towards another.

Although the Polaire Rule was bound by time and place, it is a fine Rule and the spirit of it is retained. The Lodge also inherited from the Polaires the following words, said to be 'of oriental origin'. (I have modified the gender-specific pronouns, just as I have in the White Eagle quotations in this book.) I focus on the words because I think they will eventually amplify for us the

*1 Corinthians 2 : 9; Luke 23 : 43.     †For the Polaires, see p. 147.

ways in which 'brotherhood' can be realized and the idea of 'the blooming of the Rose' understood.

*Speak to your brother or sister of the aim you have in common. Sympathize with their sufferings and share their joys— share all three with them. But be blind, dumb and deaf to all outside this triangle of the brotherhood of spirit.*

Although the words may be interpreted specifically to exclude gossip and tittle-tattle, they clearly go deeper. What, in particular, is the meaning of the phrase 'All outside this triangle of the brotherhood of spirit'? Is it only gossip that is excluded?

Whenever I put the question to myself, the answer that comes back is a surprisingly uncompromising one: *every* remark that does not put first the kinship we have to our brother–sister is outside the triangle. Every single being has first of all to be identified with and loved, because in essence they are the same as ourselves. There is no place within the 'Rule' of the Lodge for judging another human being in the slightest way: absolutely none at all.

This notion has been a part of Christian teaching from the outset, but it has become very easy to think of it as relative. While we may try hard to forgive someone we know and like for an unexpected lapse, others such as the war criminal or an individual society regards as utterly depraved may seem to be beyond the pale of understanding. Actually, the rule of brotherhood includes every one of them. Sometimes an effort of real imagination and understanding is required to develop the sympathies enough to remember that those that society rejects are made of exactly the same stuff as we are made. We do not have to forgive what people *do*, of course. We do not have even to *like* them. It is their inward selves that we need to be able to see, through the outer cloak. We can link ourselves to their inner selves again, as brothers and as sisters.

Once White Eagle was asked by a student whether what he had heard was true, that what Jesus taught was really for the next age, the Aquarian, rather than for the one which we have now more or less left. Without in any way intending to dismiss the power that Christianity has had for good over the last two thousand years, he said, 'In one sense what the questioner says is right—that is, the religion of Christ taught by Jesus is the religion of the Aquarian Age because it is a religion of love and brotherhood'. More than once White Eagle reminds us that we have only *begun* to grasp the meaning of Jesus's teaching. The ideal of the Brotherhood may sound difficult to rise to, but White Eagle's teaching helps by offering us a way of achieving our ideal, a way which is based on simplicity: by making a simple contrast between living out of our fears, and living by the law of love.

I will try and put this in the context of everyday life and its problems. All we really have to do is to remember that it is always the finite mind that throws up our fears, though the imagination then gives them shape. We fear that unless we condemn the wrongdoer, the wrong will be repeated; that unless we strike first, another will hurt us; that unless we speak out, we are guilty by association, and so on. Fair enough; we actually *do* feel angry, outraged, scandalized. Yet the enemies we imagine, or the people we blame, are not necessarily the right ones. All these feelings are quite appropriate to attach to the crime itself. Yet the crime and the wrongdoer are different: whatever the magnitude of his or her crime, the wrongdoer has within them the same seed of God as we have. If we are centred in our true being neither can the fear of the deed touch us, nor (since we acknowledge the uniqueness of their karma) will we mistake the person for the crime. To contact our own inner Christ, our light within, in absolute simplicity, is actually to contact the Christ within the other person. A real increase in understanding then occurs.

There is no difference from the act of self-forgiveness, when we lay judgment aside and open our hearts to the loving light of the universe, in the way this process works. In the *mind* we might seek to condemn ourselves or others: opening the heart takes away the need to judge or, if we have already judged, helps us overturn this judgment by forgiving. Opening the heart opens us to existence itself, unlimited, not defined in any way. In that state, *because* there are no labels or categories, we are restored to our full value as something no different either from each other, or from God.

White Eagle's teaching is one of absolute happiness. The opening of the heart is *magical* in its depth. It can also be quite instantaneous. That is why, just now, in describing the moments when we rediscover our fundamental connection with the source of things I included the process of being in love in the romantic sense. Although falling in love is often seen as akin to a social disability, it is in truth a psychic and emotional process of tremendous depth and huge growth in imaginative awareness. All of a sudden, every little detail about another person which we would have questioned before, we suddenly *love*. We forgive them everything, because in a non-intellectual way we suddenly have an understanding of their motivation.

Truly to be open in one's heart is to be in love all the time, but with everyone, most of all our own being, and *without any fear* of the consequences. This is why happiness, not moral worthiness, is the watchword in following the White Eagle path of brotherhood and spiritual unfoldment. It may sound like hedonism, but I must stand by the concept. Deeply, attachment to spirit is not attachment to morality. But neither is it remotely irresponsible. What we follow fearlessly is our dharma, our path, not our emotional whims. I think the following words attributed to White Eagle in Minesta's memoir THE ILLUMINED ONES (p.

19) help to define the power I give to happiness.

*Heaven is a state of conscious happiness, realized in different degrees in the soul. It is anywhere where you are happy according to the measure of your consciousness. You may think that heaven is a long way off, but God meant that men and women should live in heaven while still on earth.*

He goes on to remind Minesta that humanity was born to bliss, and yet, as he says, men and women have 'lost the secret' of it. She asks whether they will find it again, and he says:

*They will. But only through the pain and the joy that human love brings.*

When I say we need to be in love all the time 'without any fear of the consequences', therefore, I do not mean to imply license, but that when we work from the heart we are working from our true selves. One of the indications of real contact with the heart is that then the fears to which the outer self, the mind self, is prone, do not dominate us. The true self knows that it is imperishable and cannot be touched by misfortune, the behaviour of others, or disease, age and death. Therefore, when we truly contact our selves, other people's actions and attitudes, even if they seem malign, do not affect us. We still know that they are 'wrong' because we see that they are the other person's acts of fear, but we recognize that their fear is not cured by our antagonism or by our fear in return. We recognize fear in another for what it is—only a response to a danger which they perceive—and we do not feel the need to retreat into our own fears to respond. Not being fear-bound ourselves, we feel strength. We not only know that all is well, but by the conscious act of being our true selves we are even in that moment radiating light, *creating* good, because the only thing a light can do is to shine. This way, to echo the biblical phrase, we bring our light into the darkness, every time we refocus upon our inner being.

Happiness is not only what comes to us when we recognize the light in ourselves, it is also a good rule of thumb by which to be sure that what we have found really *is* the light, when we believe we have found it. If there is real happiness in something, there is, in some measure, truth. Happiness is not over-excitement, or indulgence, and is never the pretence of itself, never contrived for effect, but something in the consciousness which we recognize when we look inwards. Happiness is so simple that it is most easily discovered when we stop for a moment and become quite spontaneous. That spontaneity might express itself as a sigh of recognition, a sudden acknowledgment of the ridiculousness of outward events, or as an awareness of beauty, or love for another, previously unnoticed. This is happiness which we allow to come from within, and it is a point of contact with our own truth.

In chapter four I mentioned the power of simply listening. The inspiration for this remark lay in a passage of White Eagle's teaching in THE WAY OF THE SUN (pp. 39–40):

*If you could but give yourselves time to withdraw from the outer or material planes of life, and* listen! *When sitting at peace in your garden, or walking in the open places within your towns, or in quiet country lanes, give yourselves time to listen to the voice of love, which will then surely make itself known in the quiet of your soul.... Cultivate the art of listening, in your quiet moments, to the spirit, and it will speak ever in one language, that of love. Love brings to your heart peace, kindliness, tolerance, a desire to forget selfish aims, and a longing to give that which your spirit has revealed to you, to the rest of humanity.*

Remembering our happiness is very like this. There is a delightful simplicity about White Eagle's teaching; in many ways it consists only in trusting moments of natural contentment and allowing them to happen as often as possible by not stifling them. The virtue he advocates most often is simply kindness. When we are happy, it is when we act not from our social conditioning (which is unconsciously) but from our hearts; for as it is the location of spirit, the heart is full of happiness. Through happiness the ideal of brotherhood is strengthened in the world.

Without a lot of intellectual structure, the White Eagle way is to live consciously in touch with our inner light, and by so doing demonstrate the truth that all beings are spirit.

## The process of change

Actually, in spite of its simplicity, that way is quite revolutionary in its implications: much more so than people often realize. White Eagle says that knowledge of the spirit is not only a recognition but an active principle bringing about physical change:

*You are here to use physical matter, and not allow it to dominate you. You are here; you are light; and you have to shine out through the darkness. You have to use your physical life and raise it, to transmute the heavy atoms of the physical body.*

THE SOURCE OF ALL OUR STRENGTH, p. 29

It is easiest to get a clue of how this is to be done when White Eagle talks about healing:

*Within you lies the power to change the very atoms of your body, for the physical atoms are the spiritual atoms. These tiny sparks of light are the power behind all visible form. These atoms can be changed by the command of God. The whole of life is under the direction and command of the great white light.*

Stella Polaris, vol. 45 (1995–96), p. 85

What I believe White Eagle is saying is that each one of us has, within, the power of self-healing; and not only in the context of curing ourselves of a particular illness, but to the extent of rising

to a level above *all* illness. It becomes more clear that 'to see
with the eyes of the spirit' is a very radical principle. Not only is
it a tool in understanding our lives and recognizing the truth
within other people, but to see with the eyes of the spirit is to
see ourselves so radiant with light that there is no room for darkness or disease—and to know that through holding this vision
we actually *create* the beauty which we see and project.

White Eagle tells us that we ourselves change as our perspective on life develops. In chapter six of HEAL THYSELF, he explains
that earthly experience enables us slowly to develop 'higher'
bodies around our physical one, in which we can function. It is
'through discipline and initiation' that we develop first of all our
emotional, and then mental and etheric bodies in daily life. Later,
the celestial or causal body, the highest vehicle of being, develops. 'Discipline', I suspect, is best seen as a process of getting on
with the task in hand—keeping our vision focused—rather than
self-criticism and correction. 'Initiation' is what life brings us,
and White Eagle is very clear that initiation is an expansion of
consciousness at an inner level, not always a visible milestone on
the outer plane. Often the word is used in the context of what
may seem like cataclysmic change; but in truth, he says, all life is
initiation and every moment of it takes us forward. It therefore
serves us well to focus utterly on the moment, every moment.

The arresting point of White Eagle's teaching here is that if
we do not continue to sow the seeds of death in our selves, we
shall not die. The seeds of death are our ever-present existential
fears, our fears about our health, and our fears of unhappiness
and unfulfilment: our fears about death itself (remember the
phrase 'the mad fear of death', in chapter two). They manifest
not only in illness directly, but in all the things which through
conditioning we do out of fear. We may choose the wrong diet,
overstrain our bodies and nervous systems, damage ourselves

with nicotine and all sorts of other drugs; act retributively or in revenge; restrict and define our lives; criticize and chastise ourselves; believe we are incapable. This is why the process actually does take a long time: in truth, all those fears are very deeply held in us. Earth actually *is* a very hard place to be, a 'dark planet' in one sense, a severe schoolroom; but in the moment that we 'see with the eyes of spirit', the fears vanish. Constantly we rise up triumphant over earthly darkness, and yet again by the nature of life we are brought down. Thus there is no substitute for steady soul work, spiritual work.

White Eagle teaches that there is no better or faster road for this than the path of service. This is something already discussed under the third Principle of the Lodge, but perhaps it now becomes more clearly understood. The work, for instance, of participating in a White Eagle healing group, projecting light to a number of patients who have sought help, is a discipline which reminds us constantly of the power of spirit—in our own lives as well as in other people's. Every now and again we see miracles happening, and that is a reminder of the magical power of spirit.

Slowly, through this prolonged but specific focusing, the power of the light becomes real. I speak from deep experience here: years ago when I began to sit on an absent healing group, I expected sooner or later to have clear indications of what it can do in others through the results that were being reported. I did not imagine that my first evidence of its power would be discovered in myself. It is a warmth found within, a continuing sense of open-heartedness and therefore an openness to love in both general and specific manifestation. So, I feel sure, comes the time when we are—through practice, and at last—truly allowing the light to operate through us. Many Indian and new age teachings speak of opening the chakras or energy centres in the body or allowing the kundalini energy to rise from the base of the spine.

White Eagle states quite categorically that the only thing we need to do is to work always and constantly from the heart centre: that is, from our consciousness of love, as we do in the healing work. Then *all* the chakras are under the control of the divine will and all can open 'as flowers to the sunlight' safely and easily. *In the White Eagle Lodge we work on one specific ray to help each other rise above the limitations of the earth. Step by step this is taking place, but so imperceptibly in us all that it is not apparent, except perhaps in the atmosphere (which may be felt as a loving atmosphere), because the one foundation on which the God-powers can be built is that of devotion, of love.... Through these the heart chakra opens and the light streams forth from the heart.... The light from the heart stimulates the serpent power, the creative power, and as this power rises it stimulates all the other centres of the body.*

Unpublished teaching of December 1942

The heart is the way to all power, for it is the way to the Christ within.

In the chapter in HEAL THYSELF, just mentioned, White Eagle uses the word 'ascension', one much used today to imply that we can take ourselves, bodies and all, into an arisen state, through short but intense spiritual practice. The full quotation appears on the next page. The difference in emphasis in White Eagle's teaching from some teachers who have used the word extensively is that he says this is to be done by all of us, but only through the absolute blossoming of divine love within the being. There must be no attachment, no fear, no doubt whatsoever; and that does not mean it is to be attained by an effort of will, but rather through a steady process of eradication of fear through the incoming of love: an *absolute confidence* that all is good.

Only everyday life teaches this, he says. To reach the moment of ascension—that is, to leave the cycle of rebirth—does not really require particular practices. Meditation helps and so does the service of healing—but it is the absolutely natural outcome of incarnation for every person upon earth. It can be speeded up in the sense that 'seeing with the eyes of spirit' is a conscious choice to be made over and over again, but it is not something that can be hurried in any other sense. One of White Eagle's sayings is that no spiritual train will ever leave without you. To want to hurry the divine process implies a certain fear: a fear that unless things happen at once we may lose sight of them and fall into the abyss. That fear too has to be overcome.

When he talks of developing the higher bodies White Eagle also refers to the 'higher self'. This is a related concept, although the higher self is not so much something we develop as something which already exists and can be contacted in ordinary life as deeper wisdom. In the chapter mentioned from HEAL THYSELF he says that 'the higher self ... is pulsating with light, which as you develop will begin to shine through the chakras in the etheric body, the windows of your soul'. This is the process described by the Lodge's symbol of the six-pointed Star, when the higher self, as the downward-pointing triangle, is manifested in and upon the upward-pointing one—the aspiring soul. What happens, I suspect, is that the more we allow the consciousness of the light within, the more we actually function from a higher consciousness and with a better viewpoint. Whether or not the earth changes, our perception of it changes, and what once seemed to be feared becomes loved, what seemed ugly slowly becomes beautiful. There is no waste in the divine plan: all is reclaimed, regenerated, *good*. White Eagle therefore says that when the whole body is radiant with light it

*will be in a state of ascension. We mean by this that the whole body, although still of a physical nature, will be functioning on a much higher plane of consciousness than it is at present....*

*The body will be quickened in vibration and will be light and beautiful....*

HEAL THYSELF, pp. 48–49

All this is mystery, albeit beautiful mystery. My own purpose in writing is simply to give encouragement and to say that I believe the vision of the Lodge *works*. People do change. Truly to see with the eyes of spirit does bring a massive alteration of perspective to the life, and it does eventually bring change to the body. White Eagle says that through the spirit vision you

*discover that there is something finer, nobler, grander, more lovely and beautiful to live for.... Then you will no longer grow weary but be full of joy.... Oh, life is grand, my children, for those who have attained freedom in spirit!*

Talk at the Silver Jubilee of the Lodge, 22nd February 1961

There is a further level at which the concept of brotherhood resonates in White Eagle's teaching, and that is the work of the brotherhood in spirit. You will recall that I spoke of the brotherhood as being timeless, those on earth today being merely an episode in a much vaster sequence. The brotherhood in spirit are referred to often in White Eagle's teaching. It is a hopeful teaching, for one of the inferences is that when we ourselves have completed our present life we can actually continue to be of use and service to those who remain, in particular to those we have personally loved. This is how White Eagle explains his own role: one who has walked before in shoes like ours, maybe even with us, and humbly offers advice from his higher perspective.

Yet he implies rather more than this: namely, the existence of an identifiable group of spirit beings who have taken on the task of showing to humanity again and again over the ages the truth, constantly putting reminders before it. Sometimes these teachers act through a physical body. Sometimes we know their names, and sometimes not at all, for on earth they work as often in anonymity as in positions of prominence. Or they may work simply from what White Eagle calls 'the Christ-Star circle' in the world of spirit where the blueprint for humanity's evolution is hatched. At all events they work lovingly, selflessly. It is difficult not to call them 'the White Brotherhood' for they are absolutely suffused with light in precisely the way that White Eagle describes (in the passage from HEAL THYSELF) and thus they do appear to be white, but we tend to call them the higher Star Brotherhood, those in whom the six-pointed Star is manifest.

In promoting this concept of a discarnate brotherhood, White Eagle has no desire to overawe, or to belittle the human. He is indeed, as so often he is called, simply 'the gentle brother', the one who inspires and encourages, and never judges or condemns. Nor do any of the brothers in the world of spirit. They look gently on human kind and with great love, and remind them periodically of their own presence, thus giving them the hope that it is possible to rise and to transcend limitation. You may recall the words of White Eagle's I quoted at the beginning (p. 29: 'We are spiritual beings, even as you are also spirit—you manifest through the flesh, we are of the unseen, yet lent the power to make ourselves manifest and audible to you'.

The work of human development is unfinished, indeed hardly begun. Many roads may have to be followed; many strange ones too, if the sympathies are going to be developed. For some time indeed—I hope a long time, for it is a happy path—you may be conscious of White Eagle as your teacher. You may, at a level a little beneath the everyday consciousness, recognize him and the workers in the spirit who are his companions; and you may in the future, perhaps where names and outward personalities seem entirely different, recognize the warm clasp of an old friend.

# A profile of the White Eagle Lodge

### 1. When and where did the White Eagle Lodge begin?

The Lodge first opened in Kensington, London, in 1936, as a platform from which White Eagle's teaching could be heard. The work of the inner Brotherhood, however, goes back to 1934. The original group met as the English wing of a French mystical brotherhood inspired, similarly, by brethren 'within the world of light'. It was called La Fraternité des Polaires, and we have already touched on them (pp. 80, 134). Their symbol was the six-pointed Star, used by the Lodge as a symbol to this day, and their work was similar. Early in 1935, at White Eagle's direction, the English group severed its links with the French, whose later history is obscured by the wartime occupation of Paris.

Another great influence upon the new Lodge was the example and posthumous teaching of the English Spiritualist Sir Arthur Conan Doyle (creator of Sherlock Holmes and other heroes) who gave clear evidence of 'coming back' shortly after his passing in 1930, with the aid of the Polaires, in order to give a series of messages through Grace Cooke. These messages substantially amended the formal tenets of Spiritualism and are one of the foundations of the teaching in the Lodge today.*

After a period of about two years during which the group met at Burstow Manor, near Horley in Surrey, White Eagle gave instruction that the time was right for the formation of an organization in an urban situation. And so on 22nd February 1936 the Lodge opened, in London and (more or less simultaneously) in Edinburgh. Only four years later it was to suffer the loss of its London premises in an air raid. However, with the Edinburgh group still functioning, and those in London strong enough to rally round, it was still active in its work at an inner and outer level to overcome fear and provide healing and renewed vision for people throughout the war. It opened in new premises, still in Kensington, only six months after the bombing. Towards the end of war, White Eagle instructed his medium to open a retreat home outside London. That home, New Lands, near Liss in Hampshire, was dedicated on 29th September 1945.

The Mother Lodge centres upon these two sites. The first overseas Daughter Lodge was founded a decade later at May's Landing, New Jersey, USA, in 1947. Nowadays there are seventeen Daughter Lodges globally and will shortly be nineteen.

Overall, the development of the Lodge has come about through step-by-step guidance from spirit revealed in different places and at different times, but with remarkable continuity. Inevitably the Lodge has its own extraordinary history, much enshrined in the memories of its members (and told, as far as 1986, in the book THE STORY OF THE WHITE EAGLE LODGE). This story, in my opinion, is one of rich indebtedness to selfless service by many, many people who promoted the work with their time and material resources, both in the early days and since, to give it the character it has today. The guidance which has brought

*See the account given in ARTHUR CONAN DOYLE'S BOOK OF THE BEYOND.

the Lodge this far has been revealed slowly and there is undoubtedly further work for it, yet to unfold.

## 2. A growing worldwide family

Although it would be easy to overemphasize the concept of family, the extent to which it is emphasized at all in the Lodge symbolizes very clearly how much the vision of the Lodge is to function by the strength of personal relationships more than by the structure of organization.

The only title which Grace Cooke permitted herself was that of Mother of the Lodge. This name was eventually passed on jointly to her two daughters Joan Hodgson (1913-1995) and Ylana Hayward. Both of them have been intimately associated with the compilation of the White Eagle books as well as in the direction of the Lodge, and the role of Mother is that of guardian of the vision as well as leader.

The development of the Lodge has been organic, and the principal way it has grown as an organization is through its many informal groups across the world, and the way in which they form such a widespread mutuality. Members of the groups generally study the White Eagle teachings, participate in the healing work or meditate together. Many people have commented on how visiting another group of Lodge people is like coming into the same family, whether it is in the same country or somewhere round the world.

White Eagle's teaching seems to translate easily into most of the European languages. The first translations of the books took place in the Netherlands and Switzerland. Nowadays most of them are available in Dutch, Danish, German and Swedish, and some in Italian, Spanish, Portuguese, French, Norwegian, Finnish, Czech, Hebrew, Japanese, Serbo-Croat, and Turkish. There are substantial groups of White Eagle's followers in most countries in Northern Europe. There are established White Eagle centres in Sweden (with a retreat centre near Gothenburg), Denmark, the Netherlands, Germany and Switzerland. Smaller groups operate in Belgium, Norway, Italy, France and Portugal.

Outside Europe the Lodge is principally known in the English-speaking world, although there are small groups in South and Central America and White Eagle's teaching is popular in Japan. The first Temple of the White Eagle Lodge outside the United Kingdom was opened in Australia at Maleny, Queensland, in September 1990. As well as having a strong local following, Willomee (the name given to the centre as a whole) acts as a place of Retreat for the whole of Australasia. It is run by an enthusiastic team with a family at its heart. Doris and Alf Commins were its founders, and the younger generation of their family carry it forward. Willomee is typical of White Eagle Lodges in that much of the work is done by volunteers, both outside and in—landscaping, gardening, catering, clerical, secretarial, as well as the work of healing service. The site of the Temple on one of the hills of the Coastal Ranges is believed to have been an aboriginal gathering-place in years gone by; it seems to maintain that aura of sacredness today. Willomee is called after the valley in the Andes which Minesta describes in THE ILLUMINED ONES.

Since 1993 there has been a White Eagle Daughter Lodge in Melbourne, and one in Sydney is due to be dedicated. There are groups in New Zealand, while those in South Africa are linked by the leader in Cape Town, and there have been groups in Ghana, Nigeria and Cameroon for a number of years.

In North America enthusiastic groups have met for some time right across the continent from British Columbia to Quebec, from California to Massachusetts, and from Minnesota down to Florida. Since 1986, these groups have looked to the Lodge in

Montgomery, Texas, as their continental centre, though there are also Daughter Lodges in Los Angeles and in Ontario; and a real sense of creative diversity across the continent will strike anyone who visits. Montgomery, about an hour and a half's drive north of Houston, was chosen both intuitively and for its half-way position between the east and west coasts by Jean Le Fevre, a very trusted friend and helper who (like Doris Commins, in Australasia) has the role of Mother of the work in the Americas. She is assisted by her husband John and by her untiring helper Brother Lawrence, as well as a very hard-working team of volunteers and paid staff. Through the efforts of Jean and her team, and under White Eagle's guidance and inspiration, the third White Eagle Temple was opened there in October 1992. A purpose-built Retreat Center building is due to follow early in 2000.

St John's Retreat Center, as the Montgomery Lodge is known, holds retreats on special subjects including ecological awareness. It has a record of association with the Native American tradition in its modern as well as ancient form. Jean is initiated into the Wolf Clan Medicine Lodge of the Seneca and was appointed a Peace Elder at the Wolf Song gathering in 1990.

All the centres offer a full programme of White Eagle activities as well as the retreats mentioned, and they generally have opportunities for volunteer work also.

I should like to share two records, one historical, the other more contemporary, which illustrate in a human way how the Lodge functions and is supported round the world. The first is taken from the Lodge magazine in November 1947 and describes the first White Eagle Daughter Lodge to be founded outside the United Kingdom (the word 'temple' is, incidentally, a misnomer in comparison with more recent developments, but the little Lodge, now closed, will always be the root of the American work):

*Friends of the White Eagle Lodges in Britain will be interested to hear that a Daughter Lodge has been opened in America—the first to be built in that country.*

*The founder is a Mrs Robinson, who, whilst on a short visit to England last year, attended a service at the London Lodge, and from that moment was inspired to carry White Eagle's teaching to the States and to found a Lodge in New Jersey. The result is a veritable proof of unwavering faith, courage and selfless service on her part and that of her husband, who, starting with no material help, but guided and supported from the inner planes, planned and worked and brought into being the beautiful little temple now dedicated to the work.*

*The building, comprising the chapel, healing rooms and offices, was constructed single-handed by Mr Robinson—even to the cutting of the timber and making of the concrete blocks of which the walls are built, the installing of electric light and the plumbing. Working steadily from 4 am each day throughout the intense heat of the summer [he made sure that] the building gradually took shape and was completed by the opening date, August 17th, 1947.*

*Two members from the Mother Lodge who happened to be in America at the time attended the dedication and were much impressed by the power filling the chapel during the beautiful service, and also by the number of people who came to hear White Eagle's teaching. This appeared remarkable as the Lodge is situated in the woods of New Jersey, 16 miles from the nearest town and the community is widely scattered. Yet of that same community very many are seekers of the truth and have become members. Already healing and meditation groups have been started, as well as a group for spiritual unfoldment.*

In the second item, from the Lodge journal thirty-nine years later, our 'Mother' for Australasia described the delightful but sometimes daunting task which she and her family face today:

*The work in Australia continues to grow slowly but steadily. My daughters Gay and Lyn have just returned from visiting our groups in Perth and Adelaide. Gay writes: 'Under the aura and protection of the majestic, towering Ghost Gum trees, White Eagle's Western Australian family gathered to commence the mini-retreat. It was immediately apparent that we were meeting old friends!'*

*And one of the group leaders in Western Australia, who was hosting the event, comments: 'Very quickly the retreat centre filled with the light of angels, which spread like liquid gold through the hearts and minds of the members. Monday evening was particularly special as we all felt Minesta's and Brother Faithful's presence very strongly and their keen interest in the work here. Grace and Ivan Cooke were in Harvey in 1922–23 and it is the group's pipedream to have a weekend retreat centre in the area of Harvey, or at least sow the seeds of the possibility, preferably in this lifetime(!)'.*

*Gay continues: 'Then, as if carried on eagle's wings, we arrived in Adelaide to the overwhelming warm welcome of our dear family there. However different the retreats were, there were always the common denominators of love, brotherhood, sharing and caring, and lots and lots of laughter!'.*

The report continues, covering all the Australian and New Zealand groups, and Doris adds:

*Do you know, the most heartwarming thing about being in the Lodge is that no matter where one goes there is always that bond of brotherhood, the love which links us all together heart to heart?*

*Life at the Temple here is not all hard work, although we have the full complement of services—absent healing groups each day of the week, contact healing services, retreat weeks, public services, meditation groups, and book study courses, not to mention a very popular vegetarian cookery class (particularly as we get to eat the cooking!). Once a year we let our hair down at our Fancy Dress Party. What a ball we have! What do we do on nights like this? Come on over and see, and join in the fun and laughter!*

### 3.  And what about the United Kingdom?

Along with Edinburgh, already listed, there are currently White Eagle Daughter Lodges in Glasgow, Leeds, Ipswich, Reading, Bournemouth, and Teignmouth/Exeter. The Lodge described as being at 'Crowborough and Brighton' actually operates over a wide area and currently holds activities in Tunbridge Wells, Eastbourne and Worthing as well as Crowborough and Brighton. There are groups throughout the United Kingdom from the north of Scotland to Cornwall; the list is ever-changing.

The historical centre of the work remains the Mother Lodge, with its twin nuclei the London Lodge in Kensington and the Temple and retreat home at New Lands. The majority of the administrative work of the Lodge is now done from New Lands, which tends to be the centre to which people come for extended focus on the teaching. London has similar activities, but is more frequently a gateway for people into the Lodge, either as their first point of contact or if, for instance, they are visiting from outside the United Kingdom. The London Lodge underwent a transformational refurbishment in the mid-1990s: it reopened in January 1996 after a six-month closure. The underlying purpose was to allow the work to move forward in line with the changing needs of a centre in a city, a centre which anyone may drop into during opening hours. This has enhanced its 'gateway' role, though the inner work is the same here as throughout the Lodge worldwide. Activities each week include forty-one absent healing groups, including one conducted in French and one for animal patients, four contact healing services, a service of worship and communion, and two meditation groups. A number of less frequent activities such as discussions, one-day and two-day courses, yoga classes and lectures complete the programme. There is an occasional drama group and collaboration with New Lands in outdoor activities which stretch from gardening to hiking.

New Lands, as the country centre, has a programme which often emphasizes slow and full assimilation of the teaching within a peaceful and unpressurized atmosphere. For this reason the retreats are a central feature; but there is also a fortnightly Sunday Service, a monthly meditation, three contact healing services a week and approximately twenty-five absent healing groups. There are activities for children. In New Lands and in London alike, there are services of rededication for healers and further regular meditation groups following training, and the training of healers is largely done here. There are several yoga classes and a counselling support group. New Lands offers the scope to develop all sorts of ways of putting the teaching into practice, and the result is that the range of activities is diverse. For instance, we are engaged in developing the land organically and in exploring the inner life of nature in themed retreats.

The White Eagle School of Astrology operates from New Lands and holds activities there, in London, and at various Daughter Lodges worldwide. Inaugurated in 1976 and founded under White Eagle's guidance by Joan Hodgson, the School offers astrological readings as well as training . Its fully-accredited courses in esoteric astrology are unique. It has a biannual magazine, *Altair*. The Principal is Simon Bentley. One of its current projects is the creation of a specialist astrological library, at the London Lodge, which will be a facility with few rivals in the United Kingdom, although the general esoteric lending libraries at New Lands and in London are long-established and much used.

The Mother Lodge fulfils a dual function. In one respect it is the Lodge for two local communities and the principal centre in the United Kingdom. In another, and in a way that is intended entirely to transcend national boundaries and identities, it is the overall centre of the White Eagle Lodge and provides leadership and training to the groups and centres in the rest of the world. Retreats are often international in flavour and New Lands is equipped to bring members from all over the world together in conference. As the administrative centre it relies on a staff of both volunteers and paid helpers, all of whom give generously of their time; it is also the centre for the distribution of the published teaching. Volunteer workers are normally welcomed at all the major White Eagle centres.

## 4. The Lodge and the natural world

One of the respects in which White Eagle's American Indian presence is reflected in the typical lifestyle of the Lodge membership is in a sense of closeness to the natural world and of its sacredness. White Eagle teaches us to walk lightly on Mother Earth: this implies a nonviolent attitude to the world, where everyone does their best not to add more than necessary to the levels of pollution and waste. Such a determination is entirely up to the individual member, but the consciousness of the earth's needs as a whole permeates White Eagle's teaching, perhaps from its Native American influences. A nonviolent approach suggests vegetarianism, which is normal in the Lodge, although there are many members who do eat meat. At levels of closer involvement, greater strictness in diet *is* asked of participants.

The idea of closeness to the natural world obviously underlies the choice of a country centre like New Lands. On retreats, it is the external natural world as well as the inner world that is enjoyed. Through quiet observation and listening, communion with both is possible. White Eagle's guidance has been felt in the siting of all three major centres for his work: the temples are each an hour or so from a major city, on land little disturbed by recent settlement but offering signs of ancient worship.

New Lands is set in twenty-five acres of garden and agricultural land upon the sandy ridges between the North and South Downs. Work parties help in the upkeep of this land, and an increasing amount of home-grown produce is used in catering there. The Temple at Maleny, also, is surrounded by farmland and enjoys an inspiring view across a valley towards further hills. A small creek rises below the Temple and flows into rainforest in the valley below. The land on the ridge is farmed but the Temple garden has been beautifully developed by helpers. St John's Retreat Center in Texas is on a tract cleared from the edge of the old American 'great thicket' and draws much of its magical beauty from the land that surrounds it. Circles of pine trees grace the higher parts of the land and there are fine oaks and other trees. An artificial lake offers a symbol for meditation. There is a small creek running through the seventy or so acres of land.

In Texas as at the Australasian centre there has been a degree of pioneering to draw land which inherently has all the dangers of the wild into a place of community between people and nature. It seems to have been the special task of 'St John's' to put into full practice what White Eagle teaches about the natural world—to respect it and to love it, and slowly to assist in establishing harmony between earth, animals and human beings. It is common for retreat participants to get caught up in enthusiasm for the beauty of the land and its creatures! The feeling of pioneering community draws visitors to Texas from the Lodge all over the world. Jean's work, which began in the animal welfare movement, has led to a specialization in the rehabilitation of injured wild birds, particularly raptors, and has been a particular inspiration within and outside the White Eagle work.

At St John's Retreat Center there is opportunity for study of the rituals of the Native Americans, which develop for us a sense of the sacredness of things. Such knowledge can be a beautiful extension to the simple White Eagle way. It is recognized that there is a propriety to all of the rituals both in the sense of what is appropriate and what is the preserve of the Native Americans themselves. A balance in this as in all things is necessary, and constantly needs to be redefined: this finding of balance is something that runs right through White Eagle's teaching.

## 5. The history of the healing work

Today the healing work in the Lodge is long-established, and further requirements in professional training are regularly applied, partly to fulfil ongoing agreements with the Confederation of Healing Organizations, of which the Lodge in the United Kingdom is a member.

Yet the healing work in the Lodge was instituted from the very beginning, in 1936, and followed White Eagle's precise instructions. At the same time it owes a very great deal to Ivan Cooke, who himself was a remarkable healer; and also to the careful guidance of Joan Hodgson, who built upon the pioneering work he did and was Healing Secretary to the Lodge for a great many years.

One of the things White Eagle gave was a form of service for healing which involved six sitters meeting in a circle and projecting healing light ('thoughts' or 'prayers' are also appropriate words) in the form of colour rays to the patient, who in this form of healing is not physically present. The first such 'absent healing' groups were formed in 1936; by the outbreak of the war there were five and today there are over 250 groups throughout the world. There are also groups of 'lone healers': that is, those who work from their own homes and not in an actual White Eagle centre or Lodge. Beyond this, there is a form of 'contact healing' taught in the Lodge, contact healing being used when the patient prefers to be physically present; it normally takes place in an actual service, when there are a number of patients gathered and the words of the service help them make their inner contact beforehand.

Joan Hodgson wrote the following words about the healing: *Many people feel they need some special magnetic power to be a healer; certainly some have this gift and can use it effectively, but this is not an essential for true spiritual healing. Everyone has within their heart the spark of Christ light which can be strengthened and made more active, and through this they can learn to direct the light of love and healing into physical matter. The White Eagle healing training helps students to unfold the power of the Christ Sun in the heart.*

Booklet, *About the White Eagle healing work*, p. 2

The Lodge healing is open to everyone, as a watching participant at a healing service, as a patient, or as a healer. Many people come just to enjoy the beauty of the contact healing service and watch while the patients are called before an altar of light and a row at a time receive their individual 'treatments' from the team of healers. Each patient has their own healer who applies the colours not only by thought-projection but through the hands as well. There are explanations of the colours in the books HEALING BY THE SPIRIT (Ivan Cooke) and A WHITE EAGLE LODGE BOOK OF HEALTH AND HEALING (Joan Hodgson).

All sorts of conditions and illnesses are treated, from exam stress to terminal illness. White Eagle, of course, would disregard the phrase 'terminal illness': from his perspective there can be no such thing. Nonetheless, the degree of support given by the healing to people in this perceived condition can be priceless. Each generation has its own illnesses: many of them today are stress-related (and thus particularly suited to spiritual healing) but people use the healing as a backup to working through problems of childhood abuse; they may be cancer sufferers or HIV patients, or people who manifest some form of psychic disorder. All information is treated in the strictest confidence, and no disease is regarded as untreatable (though some diseases lend themselves better to the absent healing because the patient's physical or mental condition may prevent them attending). *Within* the healing work, once the colour rays have been prescribed, it is not generally regarded as useful to name the disease, not only for confidentiality but because the healer's attitude toward the patient is one of wholeness, not of the impaired body or mind.

Anyone can attune themselves to receive the healing power, both through direct application to the Lodge or simply 'tuning in' at appropriate times to the power that is being sent out, for instance at the 'magical hours' (see pp. 86, 119). There is always a service at 12.00 noon in the Temple at New Lands and in the Temples in Australia and America. Those who wish can, after making the first attunement, or perhaps working with the White Eagle Star Link (see below, pp. 163–65), seek to join the large band of White Eagle healers across the world. To be an 'absent' or 'lone' healer is a simple form of service taking up to an hour of the healer's time per week.

The healing work itself is a part of the work of the inner Brotherhood of the Lodge, the Brotherhood of the Star. The work of this Brotherhood, described in chapter seven, is intrinsically the same as the healing of individuals, although done more at the world level—it is the degree of commitment that is greater. The healing groups thus become also a training stage for those who wish to go on to the Brotherhood work.

## 6. *Links with other organizations*

By policy the Lodge has no formal links with any other groups at all (except those necessary for the accreditation of its training in healing and in astrological studies), while seeking to have as many *informal* links as possible with its sister organizations. Members and enquirers come to the Lodge from all sorts of traditions and backgrounds and help to bring some of that richness into the Lodge itself. It is often asked where the White Eagle Lodge draws its members from; actually in their roots they are just as likely to be Quaker, Catholic, Anglican, Unity, Spiritualist, Jew, Theosophist or Methodist; to come from a group with special needs (we have an international group for the blind and partially-sighted); to come from (say) the animal welfare movement; to find us through a yoga teacher; they are more or less as likely to be in any walk of life as another, or to come from minority groups such as the lesbian and gay communities. There is a good cultural diversity within the work too. For many people the Lodge provides a supplementary religious environment while they continue active involvement with (for instance) a local church. Yet despite the basis of White Eagle's teaching in Christianity, it is no closer to one Christian denomination than another, and may have as many similarities with non-Christian belief systems such as Buddhism. White Eagle acknowledges the wonderful facets of the truth exemplified by the other great world teachers or enshrined in other religions such as Islam and Hinduism, Sikhism and native religions like the American, and speaks of truth as if it were the hub of a wheel, with the many religions its spokes.

The Lodge enjoys cordial relations with its sister organizations and seeks to foster these. Because much of its work is done silently one of the Lodge's aims is to provide support at the inner level for organizations working at the outer level, either to improve the consciousness or the welfare of human beings, and the welfare of the animal kingdom and the earth itself. Its workers have a tradition of quietly helping in the formation of groups working for the improvement of human or animal welfare (in the United Kingdom, the Beauty without Cruelty movement in 1967, the group Compassion in World Farming in the late 1960s, the Francis Bacon Research Trust in 1980 and, more recently, the Dove Healing Trust and the Yoga of the Heart School, are examples). However, it has no political affiliations whatsoever. The aim of an inner Brother or Sister of the Lodge is to see beyond the narrow focus of politics.

### 7.  *Membership and other involvement in the Lodge*

The concept of the Lodge as a worldwide family is not intended to bring to it any sense of inclusion and exclusion. However, those who form part of it by committed membership affect its focus and carry with that a small measure of responsibility as a result. To be a member nonetheless requires only to be able to say that you are in general harmony with White Eagle's teaching. It is worth giving a little thought to this statement and perhaps committing to a letter, with your application, a few words about your own life and what brings you to the Lodge. This ensures that the Lodge membership is always one of people, not just of entries on a computer (however enthusiastically the Lodge may embrace labour-saving technology, it likes to be able to relate to its members personally!). Becoming a member does not mean giving up affiliations to other organizations. Because the Lodge has its own material needs, a small subscription is asked of members, although for someone with limited funds this is never intended to be a barrier to joining.

The other opportunities for service described in this book,

namely the healing and the Brotherhood work, are available to members as they refine their commitment. While attending one of the Lodges, it is possible to become a White Eagle absent healer before becoming a member, but in order to be a 'lone healer' (that is, one who works outside one of the established centres) you do need to have been a member for six months because a greater degree of trust is placed on you to continue doing the work. Training for the contact healing begins with the commencement of absent healing work, but it is normal to do two years of this before participating in a specific contact healers' training course. It will be clear from this that there is not intended to be a sense of rush in any of the opportunities open to members; similarly, it is a good rule of thumb that members regard two years' service in the healing work as a necessary period of preparation and training before applying to join the White Eagle Star Brotherhood.

At the outset, and for all those who are attracted by the work of the Lodge but do not necessarily want to take on the commitment of membership, may I recommend the White Eagle Star Link, which at the time of writing is in process of formation?

White Eagle states that the work of realizing the light of the Star in our lives and projecting it to others is something in which absolutely anyone can share. Both as a means of finding self-healing, and as a healing technique for others, it can have extraordinary power, and this is something the Lodge has publicised for many years. The Star Link gives this more focus.

Here is something written about it by one of the helpers involved in setting up the scheme, the words of which I cannot really better:

*The symbol of the six-pointed star is used often by spiritual and religious organizations worldwide. Its meaning and symbolism change depending upon where and how it is used and by whom. But it is in the White Eagle work that this symbol of the Star takes on a* reality *which transcends everyday meaning, goes deeper than thought, rises above emotion and calls the individual to higher ideals of service and brotherhood....*

*In the White Eagle Lodge we respect and love the Star because we know it is more than just a symbol or a vision. We have 'experienced' it—its power, love and wisdom and its practical application in the affairs of everyday living. It is a source of strength, courage, honour and integrity. We* know *the Star and we know that it is spirit.*

*To visualize the Star with our inner vision brings us directly into contact with it, into its presence, into its heart. We make our 'link' with it on the inner planes, on the ethers. As we behold the Star in our mind's eye, its light permeates us at every level, mental, emotional and physical. The effects of this are deep and profound upon the soul, taking it into an inner communion, a unity with its source. The true union experienced is so beautiful that it cannot easily be conveyed in words.*

*The White Eagle Star Link is just this—a link—with the Star, with the world of spirit. The purpose of the Link is very simple: to spread the light of the Star that all may experience its magic, that all may benefit from being* one *under the Star.*

Participation in the work of the Star demands no formal affiliations, and while the Star Link is set up to encourage people in their focus under the Star and give them support in their continued practice of this, it is intended to run with a minimum of administration. There is a Star image in its own web site on the Internet to give a visual focus in this concentration; the address is www.thestarlink.net. Beyond this there is an occasional newsletter, readable both on the Internet and by conventional mail, and a small subscription to defray costs for those who would like to link with others through the newsletter, and with the centre of the Star Link work.

The addresses to write to for details about membership or details of the Star Link alike are those given on pp. 172-73.

## 8. How is the Lodge financed?

The Lodge is almost entirely supported by its members, friends and those who purchase its publications. Some of this support comes through direct subscription, and a rather higher proportion through donations and legacies. There are regular fund-raising activities held in support of the work throughout the world—from video dinners in Los Angeles to long-distance walks around the New Lands countryside! The fund-raising activities also provide a social focus for the Lodge and it is probably true that as many friendships accrue from them as from retreats.

The Lodge has been grateful for grants from charitable trusts in helping to fund some of its capital projects, for example, the refurbishment of the London Lodge in 1995 and the extension to the Temple eleven years earlier (built at the same time as an extension to New Lands house to increase the administrative accommodation). However, by far the greater proportion of funds has come from individuals, and in the case of some, such as the Temple at New Lands, almost entirely so. Projects like the Temples and the London refurbishment have been greatly helped by free-of-interest loans.

Beside specific fund-raising appeals there is an ongoing 'fund for the future' to which individuals and others may contribute. The Lodge aims to be a self-supporting community and the contributions of individuals form the basis for the wellbeing of the whole. Tithing is encouraged, whether at the level of the original meaning of 'tithe' (a tenth) or simply as a small fraction of the income, for this is one of the most practical demonstrations one can make of absolute support for and empathy with the work. Many of the Lodge's members, though, would find it extraordinarily difficult to make such a commitment, and give what they are able when they can. Simply giving love provides much-needed support and energy. It is the most welcome gift of all.

In accordance with the requirements of local charity law, the material affairs of the Lodge in the United Kingdom are watched over by Trustees and in the case of the Australasian and American centres by Directors. This is an important provision in controlling the use of funds and qualifies the Lodge, in countries in which it is fully registered, for tax deductions on gifts.

## 9.  *White Eagle's teaching: a reading plan*

A full catalogue of the White Eagle publications is available from its principal centres and will by its nature be more up to date than anything I can give here. I suggest asking for a copy so that the titles given below can be matched to current price and so on (the Lodge web site, mentioned on the preceding page, is also kept up to date with prices and new publications). For help in ordering the books from shops, I have quoted their ISBN (International Standard Book Number); it should however be noted that a programme is under way preparing new editions of many of the books and that when these come out the ISBNs will change. The bookseller will need the prefix 0-85487 and the four digits given after the title in the following text.

In compiling the reading plan I am responding to a number of specific requests from enquirers who wanted to know which book to get and in what order. I can only group them; you will get just as much from them if you read them in the order in which you feel drawn to them intuitively, but what I can say about them may perhaps prompt the intuition!

A good book to start with would be MORNING LIGHT (018 0), which was compiled specifically for people just setting out on 'the path'. It could well be followed by its sister volume GOLDEN HARVEST (106 3). After that you might well enjoy turning to the SPIRITUAL UNFOLDMENT series, of which there are four volumes, or at least to the first of these, which is general (012 1). Book Two (001 6) is about the nature kingdom and the subtler life within it, while Book Three (075 X) centres on the ancient mysteries and Four (078 4) on brotherhood; the last two might well be better read at a slightly later stage. In addition to the books there is a set of eight booklets, some of which have been mentioned in the text. The titles of the first six are. *(1) A Brief Outline of White Eagle's Teaching; (2) Jesus the Christ, (3) Who is White Eagle?; (4) The Five Great Laws; (5) The White Brotherhood* and *(6) Spiritual Healing.* The others are on *Health and Happiness— through the way you live* (7) and *through what you eat* (8).

For all that, literally thousands of people find the little book of White Eagle sayings entitled THE QUIET MIND (104 7) is their first introduction to the work, and it evidently serves that purpose extraordinarily well! It is available in large print too (060 1) and now has a sister volume, THE SOURCE OF ALL OUR STRENGTH (097 0). Also in this series is PRAYER IN THE NEW AGE (041 5; large print, 064 4): as well as giving prayers it contains a section on affirmations, and some teaching about making the spiritual contact and finding inner strength. Another useful beginner's book is the recent BEAUTIFUL ROAD HOME (088 1).

For many, healing is the thing that draws a person to White Eagle's teaching or the Lodge, and the classic here is White Eagle's HEAL THYSELF (107 1). There are some fuller books too: Ivan Cooke's HEALING BY THE SPIRIT (069 5) is a classic from the 1950s, but still valid; Joan Hodgson's A WHITE EAGLE BOOK OF HEALTH AND HEALING (070 9) has a substantial amount of information about matters such as the colours used in healing.

Books on meditation are quite numerous on the list. The most recent is Ylana Hayward's A WAY TO HAPPINESS (094 6) while the classic is Grace Cooke's MEDITATION (110 1). Grace Cooke also wrote THE JEWEL IN THE LOTUS (067 9); this is better read after MEDITATION. There is also a book of White Eagle readings specifically for use in meditation, with a guided visualization after each one. It is called THE STILL VOICE (049 0). Another book, not specifically on meditation but with short readings that may be useful in a similar context, is THE GENTLE BROTHER (112 8).

There are also tape cassettes giving assistance in meditation and healing. Anna Hayward's ALL IS WELL is a good start for those who would benefit from basic relaxation to start with; the rest of the tapes are by Joan Hodgson and include HOW TO ATTUNE YOURSELF TO THE WHITE EAGLE HEALING, THE LAKE OF PEACE and FINDING THE MASTER WITHIN. The White Eagle list also includes four yoga tapes by Jenny Beeken and her book YOGA OF THE HEART (080 6). Some people will come to White Eagle's teaching through a desire to find out ways of self-help and how to make a spiritual programme out of White Eagle's teaching. For this there is nothing better than Jenny Dent's A QUIET MIND COMPANION (091 1).

The three paragraphs foregoing cover specific aspects of the teaching; it is time to return to the teaching in general with a few books that would be better read by someone who has already made a start in their studies. Three books in particular cover the relation of the White Eagle teaching to the Christian gospels. JESUS TEACHER AND HEALER (065 2) will also help anyone interested in healing, while THE LIVING WORD OF ST JOHN (044 X) and THE PATH OF THE SOUL (101 2) cover the teaching about the soul and its spiritual evolution, using the life of Jesus Christ as pattern and symbol. Lastly, THE WAY OF THE SUN (055 5) covers the Christian festivals, though not exclusively: it is as much about the cycle of the seasons, and the sun ceremonies.

Another book of deeper teaching is WISDOM FROM WHITE EAGLE (098 9); the subjects are quite diverse and the book is very instructive. More specific is SUNRISE (016 6), because it is defined as a book about death and the eternal life; but it has much general appeal for anyone with the least interest in what the life beyond may be like. Anyone seeking to develop mediumistic gifts is directed to Grace Cooke's THE NEW MEDIUMSHIP (068 7).

ARTHUR CONAN DOYLE'S BOOK OF THE BEYOND (093 8) is useful both for the history of the Lodge and for the extraordinarily detailed teaching about the afterlife which Sir Arthur gave. Grace Cooke wrote most illuminating memoirs of past lives which touch most helpfully upon times in human history when spirit has been particularly close. The titles are THE ILLUMINED ONES (058 X), which covers lives in Egypt and the Andes, SUN-MEN OF THE AMERICAS (057 1), and THE LIGHT IN BRITAIN (056 3).

There are also books for children on the list, and an annual Calendar.

Lastly, books on astrology. They are all by Joan Hodgson. She wrote, in order, WISDOM IN THE STARS (030 X), ASTROLOGY THE SACRED SCIENCE (046 6), PLANETARY HARMONIES (047 4) and THE STARS AND THE CHAKRAS (100 4); the last two touch on meditation and healing respectively, while the first is the most introductory. Her little book WHY ON EARTH: THE LIGHT OF THE ANCIENT WISDOM ON MODERN PROBLEMS (043 1) is mentioned in the text and still available as this book goes to press.

As far as can be established, the earliest public messages by White Eagle were given as early as 1929* but we do not have any today bearing a date before 1932, and anything before that was probably not very substantial (there are some records of

*The evidence for this is information given by Ivan Cooke in the Lodge magazine *Angelus* in 1938.

messages given in private). The very early teachings were given at Spiritualist churches or at larger venues such as the Marylebone Spiritualist Association, and later at the healing and retreat centre, Burstow Manor, which Minesta established in 1934. The main series of teachings begins with the founding of the Lodge in 1936. Some talks were given at public services, others to smaller groups of students. They continue right through to 1976.

The first White Eagle book appeared in 1937 under the title ILLUMINATION and is a more-or-less straight transcript of a number of public addresses. Subsequent books contained teaching specifically related to the current political conditions in Europe: THE PRESENT WORLD CRISIS, WAYS OF SERVICE IN THE WORLD TODAY (a more general book) and THE WHITE BROTHERHOOD, a book about the role of the Brotherhood work in holding back the forces of darkness at the time Europe was sliding into war.*

Although White Eagle is notably lucid in all his talks, the transfer of spoken English to a readable literary style has involved some editorial work from the very beginning. Moreover, original teachings in their entirety do not necessarily form workable components in the framework of a book, and most of the White Eagle books, particularly since the mid 1950s, have been compilations of shorter passages from White Eagle talks.

Most of the editorial work at the outset was done by Grace Cooke's husband Ivan (whose distinctive turn of phrase is often recognizable therein). More recently, it has been policy to edit a little less, and some of the newer books may actually be closer to the original messages than the early ones. It is surely one of the reasons why what I call 'the White Eagle Lodge experiment' exists, to keep the teaching alive and creative in our hearts and minds, and thus keep the editing process faithful and yet con-

*None of the books in this paragraph is in print. Nor are Minesta's PLUMED SERPENT and THE SHINING PRESENCE, which date from this period.

temporary. At the present moment, for instance, a programme is under way to reissue all the current books—and there are nineteen books of teaching in print in all—with corrected and revised texts that remove, as far as possible, the gender-specific pronouns with their patriarchal bias that were the norm when much of the teaching was given. This typifies the sort of work that is done editorially: the actual meaning is not intended to be changed. Because this book is written while that process is still happening, it has been difficult to know whether to quote here the unedited texts or the new ones; I have opted for an updated text, even though it may occasionally seem I have misquoted it if the text is traced back to its earlier source.

To some extent, the books I have mentioned in the text that are not specifically White Eagle books may also be ones to turn to if you would like to read something which is not part of his own teaching, but sheds light on it. While further details about the White Eagle books above are best had from The White Eagle Publishing Trust, the other books mentioned in the text are very varied, so I give full publication details in footnote form:

EMMANUEL'S BOOK and EMMANUEL'S BOOK II, New York (Bantam Books), 1985 and 1989.

Paul Beard, INNER EYE, LISTENING EAR, Norwich (Pilgrim Books), 1992; for the reader coming from Spiritualism, Paul's books are both sound and helpful.

Books by Silver Birch are published by Psychic Press, London, and available from the Psychic News Bookshop at Stansted Hall, Stansted Mountfitchet, Essex CM24 8UD.

On the Native Americans: WISDOMKEEPERS, by Steve Wall and Harvey Arden, Hillsboro, Oregon (Beyond Words Publishing), 1990, is one of many books giving teaching from present-day elders. The traditional basis for anything bringing together the Native American teachers and the traditions of the Christian world is Ernest Thompson Seton's THE GOSPEL OF THE REDMAN. The most recent reprint is by the Boy Scouts of America, 1980.

SAINT COLUMBA: edited and presented by Iain Macdonald, Edinburgh (Floris Books), 1992; ISBN 0-86315-143-4. The life of Columba mentioned is by Saint Adamnan and there are numerous full scholarly translations of the original Latin in addition to the very accessible set of excerpts in this non-specialist version. I also cited Ben Okri's article in *The Guardian* newspaper; his novels show a remarkable clear eye both in the ways I have advocated and in ways that relate specifically to the West African consciousness. RAJA YOGA by Swami Vivekananda is a classic and still widely available.

## 10. *Other information*

You may want to ask specifically for details on aspects of the Lodge work and White Eagle teaching. Before I list these, a useful resource is the Lodge's web site which is at www.whiteagle.org, while the Texas centre has a site at www.saintjohns.org. Between them, these sites list all the publications with prices and books can be ordered from them.The Star Link web site can be found at www.thestarlink.net.

The basic folder of information sent to new enquirers carries the title 'Purpose and Work'. There are specific sets of leaflets also about joining the healing work, and a folder entitled 'Using the Christ Light in Healing and Meditation' is also available.

Membership is open to all, and requires only that you are in general harmony with the teaching; you can join either by writing to the headquarters at New Lands, Brewells Lane, Liss, Hampshire, England GU33 7HY (01730 893300), or to the continental centres, namely St John's Retreat Center, 2615 St Beulah's Rd, Montgomery, Texas, U.S.A. 77316-4438 (1-409 597 5757) and Willomee, P. O. Box 225, Maleny, Queensland, Australia 4552 (07-54 944397). Any of the general information the Lodge sends you will normally give the current suggested subscription and also details of the various Daughter Lodges and the European centres, who can also handle your subscription. The Lodge e-mail address is enquiries@whiteagle.org, while the Lodge in

Texas can be reached at sjrc@saintjohns.org. The Star Link e-mail address is rays@thestarlink.net.

The magazine *Stella Polaris* is published bimonthly from New Lands and is a wonderful way to keep in touch with the Lodge, its teaching, and all its activities.

Various postal courses are available. There is a general one for members, a course in meditation, and a series of courses in astrology. These last are administered by the White Eagle School of Astrology, from the Liss address.

As an international organization the Lodge copes as best as it can with enquiries written in languages other than English; there is normally someone available to translate at least the major European languages, but write in English if you can! In the London Lodge, which probably takes more enquiries from overseas than any other of the Lodge centres, there is generally someone on hand who can speak Spanish, Italian, French or German.

A full list of groups round the world is available from Liss, on request (apply to the Americas or Australasian centres for groups in those countries).

If you would like to join an absent healing group, participate eventually as a contact healer, and perhaps have in mind to make the full commitment to the Lodge by joining the Star Brotherhood, details may be had from all the centres, including local Daughter Lodges. Remember that lone healing is an option if you live too far away from a major group to be an absent healer.

I hope the above, and all the details in the book, help you. I cannot promise to answer all queries personally, but if you find there are parts of the book that you need amplified further, or have specific questions I—and the team at the Lodge—will do our best to answer them.

# INDEX

176